SQL PERFORMANCE TUNING

TUNING

Proven Strategies for Optimizing Queries

Kiet Huynh

Table of Contents

PART I
Introduction to SQL Performance Tuning

1.1 Fundamental Concepts of SQL Performance Tuning

SQL performance tuning is a critical aspect of database management and application development. It involves optimizing the execution speed and efficiency of SQL queries to ensure that they run as fast as possible. In this section, we will explore the fundamental concepts of SQL performance tuning, laying the foundation for the rest of our journey into the world of query optimization.

Understanding SQL Performance Tuning

SQL performance tuning is the process of refining SQL queries and database operations to enhance their efficiency and speed. It's a multifaceted discipline that requires a deep understanding of how databases work, as well as the ability to analyze and improve SQL code.

Why SQL Performance Tuning Matters

SQL performance tuning is crucial for several reasons:

1. User Experience: Slow database queries can result in a poor user experience for applications and websites. Users expect fast response times, and delays can lead to frustration and abandonment.

2. Cost Savings: Inefficient SQL queries can strain hardware resources and increase infrastructure costs. By optimizing queries, you can reduce the need for expensive hardware upgrades.

3. Scalability: Well-tuned SQL queries can scale more effectively. As your application grows, optimized queries can handle increased loads without sacrificing performance.

4. Competitive Advantage: Faster applications can give your organization a competitive edge. Users are more likely to choose applications that respond quickly and reliably.

Key Components of SQL Performance Tuning

To become proficient in SQL performance tuning, you need to grasp the following key components:

1. SQL Queries: Understanding SQL query structure and syntax is essential. You must be able to read, analyze, and modify SQL queries effectively.

2. Database Structure: A solid understanding of database design, indexing, and table relationships is crucial. It helps you make informed decisions about query optimization.

3. Query Execution Plans: Query execution plans, generated by the database engine, provide insights into how queries are processed. Knowing how to interpret and optimize these plans is vital.

4. Performance Metrics: Performance metrics like execution time, CPU usage, and I/O statistics are used to evaluate query performance. Learning how to measure and interpret these metrics is fundamental.

5. Indexing Strategies: Indexes can significantly impact query performance. Understanding different types of indexes and when to use them is a critical skill.

6. Tools and Utilities: Familiarity with performance monitoring and tuning tools is essential. These tools help you identify bottlenecks and optimize queries efficiently.

7. Testing and Benchmarking: Creating realistic test environments and benchmarking query performance are essential steps in the tuning process.

Getting Started with SQL Performance Tuning

To begin your journey into SQL performance tuning, follow these initial steps:

Step 1: Learn SQL Fundamentals: Ensure you have a solid foundation in SQL. Understand basic query structure, SELECT statements, and data manipulation.

Step 2: Understand Database Basics: Familiarize yourself with database concepts such as tables, indexes, relationships, and normalization.

Step 3: Explore Query Execution Plans: Learn how to generate and analyze query execution plans using tools like SQL Server Management Studio (SSMS) or EXPLAIN in PostgreSQL.

Step 4: Identify Performance Issues: Practice identifying common performance bottlenecks in queries, such as full table scans, excessive joins, and unoptimized WHERE clauses.

Step 5: Study Indexing: Gain a deep understanding of indexes, including B-tree, hash, and bitmap indexes. Learn when and how to create them.

Step 6: Use Monitoring Tools: Experiment with monitoring tools like SQL Profiler, MySQL Performance Schema, or Oracle Enterprise Manager to capture query performance data.

Step 7: Benchmark Your Queries: Create a testing environment and benchmark your SQL queries to establish baseline performance metrics.

Step 8: Experiment and Optimize: Begin optimizing your queries by making changes to improve performance. Measure the impact of each change.

Conclusion

SQL performance tuning is a critical skill for anyone working with databases or developing applications that rely on them. This introduction provides you with a solid foundation to dive deeper into the world of query optimization. As you progress through this book, you'll learn advanced techniques, best practices, and real-world strategies for improving SQL query performance. Remember that practice and hands-on experience are key to becoming proficient in SQL performance tuning.

1.2 Why SQL Performance Tuning Matters

In today's data-driven world, where businesses rely heavily on databases to store and manage their information, the importance of SQL performance tuning cannot be overstated. It plays a pivotal role in ensuring that database systems run efficiently, delivering the best possible performance to users and minimizing operational costs. In this section, we'll explore why SQL performance tuning matters and how it impacts various aspects of an organization.

1.2.1. Enhancing User Experience

One of the primary reasons SQL performance tuning matters is its direct impact on user experience. Users have come to expect applications and websites to respond quickly and deliver content without noticeable delays. Whether it's an e-commerce platform, a social media site, or a critical enterprise application, slow response times can result in user frustration and dissatisfaction.

Consider an e-commerce website as an example. When a user searches for a product, navigates categories, or proceeds to checkout, these actions often involve complex SQL queries to retrieve relevant data from a database. If these queries are not optimized, the user may experience frustratingly slow page load times. Studies have shown that even a one-second delay in page load times can lead to a significant drop in user engagement and conversions.

In contrast, a well-tuned SQL database ensures that queries execute swiftly, delivering a seamless and responsive user experience. Users can browse products, complete transactions, and access information quickly, leading to higher customer satisfaction and retention.

1.2.2. Cost Savings

SQL performance tuning can also result in substantial cost savings for organizations. Inefficient SQL queries can place unnecessary strain on database servers, requiring more powerful and costly hardware to maintain acceptable performance levels. By optimizing queries, organizations can achieve the same or better performance with existing hardware, reducing the need for expensive upgrades.

Let's consider a scenario where an organization's database server experiences high CPU and memory utilization due to poorly optimized queries. The immediate response might be to invest in more powerful servers with additional processing power and RAM to handle the load. While this can temporarily alleviate performance issues, it's a costly solution.

SQL performance tuning offers a more cost-effective alternative. By identifying and optimizing problematic queries, organizations can reduce resource consumption, extending the lifespan of their existing infrastructure. This translates to significant cost savings in terms of hardware, energy, and maintenance.

1.2.3. Scalability

As businesses grow, their database workloads often increase. SQL performance tuning plays a crucial role in ensuring that a database system can scale effectively to accommodate growing demands. Without optimization, a database that performs adequately with a small user base may struggle to maintain performance as the number of users and data volumes expand.

Imagine a popular social networking platform that experiences rapid user growth. The SQL queries responsible for retrieving user profiles, posts, and interactions face a substantial increase in demand. Without optimization, these queries can become a bottleneck, resulting in slower response times and decreased platform reliability.

SQL performance tuning enables organizations to scale their database systems efficiently. By addressing performance bottlenecks, optimizing queries, and implementing best practices, a database can handle a larger user base and higher data volumes without sacrificing performance. This scalability is essential for businesses aiming to remain competitive in a dynamic market.

1.2.4. Competitive Advantage

In a competitive landscape, where users have a multitude of choices for applications and services, performance can be a significant differentiator. Applications that respond quickly and reliably are more likely to attract and retain users.

Consider two online retailers offering similar products and prices. One website provides near-instantaneous search results and product listings, while the other suffers from slow page load times and delays in displaying search results. Users are more likely to favor the website with superior performance, as it offers a more efficient and enjoyable shopping experience.

A competitive advantage can also be observed in the realm of enterprise applications. Businesses that leverage well-tuned SQL databases can process transactions, generate reports, and deliver insights faster than their competitors. This agility allows them to make data-driven decisions promptly, giving them an edge in the market.

1.2.5. Summary

In summary, SQL performance tuning is a critical discipline that significantly impacts various facets of an organization, including user experience, cost savings, scalability, and competitive advantage. It ensures that database systems operate efficiently, providing users with responsive applications and reducing infrastructure costs. Moreover, it enables businesses to scale their services to accommodate growth and gain a competitive edge in the market.

As we delve deeper into the world of SQL performance tuning, we'll explore the methodologies, techniques, and best practices that empower organizations to achieve these benefits and maximize the performance of their database systems. The journey begins with a solid understanding of the SQL performance tuning process, which we will explore in the next section.

1.3 Key Components of SQL Performance Tuning

SQL performance tuning is a multifaceted process that involves several key components, each contributing to the overall optimization of a database system. To effectively tune SQL performance, it's crucial to understand these components and how they interact. In this section, we'll explore the key components of SQL performance tuning and provide insights into their significance.

1.3.1. SQL Queries

At the core of SQL performance tuning are the SQL queries themselves. SQL queries are commands sent to a database to retrieve, manipulate, or modify data. These queries are constructed using SQL (Structured Query Language) and can range from simple SELECT statements to complex joins, subqueries, and updates.

Consider a scenario where a web application relies on SQL queries to display product listings to users. A poorly written query can result in slow response times, impacting the user experience. Therefore, optimizing SQL queries is often the first and most critical step in the performance tuning process.

Optimization techniques for SQL queries include:

- **Rewriting Queries:** Modifying queries to use more efficient constructs or JOIN clauses.

- **Index Utilization:** Ensuring that appropriate indexes are in place to accelerate data retrieval.

- **Parameterization:** Using parameterized queries to promote query plan reuse.

1.3.2. Database Schema Design

The database schema, which defines the structure of tables, relationships, and constraints, plays a pivotal role in SQL performance. A well-designed schema can enhance query performance, while a poorly designed one can introduce bottlenecks.

For example, in an e-commerce database, the schema should efficiently represent products, categories, and customer orders. A normalized schema minimizes data redundancy but can lead to complex JOIN operations. On the other hand, a denormalized schema simplifies queries but can result in increased storage requirements.

Database designers must strike a balance between normalization and denormalization to meet specific performance requirements. Additionally, the choice of data types, indexing strategies, and constraints all impact schema performance.

1.3.3. Indexing Strategies

Indexes are database structures that accelerate data retrieval by providing a quick lookup mechanism. They play a crucial role in SQL performance tuning. However, the effectiveness of indexing depends on various factors, including the choice of indexed columns, index type, and maintenance.

To illustrate the importance of indexing, consider a scenario where a customer database is queried based on customer names. Without an index on the name column, each query would require a full table scan, resulting in slow query performance. Implementing an index on the name column significantly improves query response times.

Common indexing strategies include:

- **B-Tree Indexes:** Suitable for equality and range queries.

- **Bitmap Indexes:** Ideal for low-cardinality columns with a limited number of distinct values.

- **Full-Text Indexes:** Used for searching within text data.

1.3.4. Query Execution Plans

A query execution plan, also known as a query plan or query optimization plan, outlines how a database engine will execute a query. It determines which tables to access, the order of table access, and the type of join operations to perform. Query execution plans are generated by the database optimizer, which strives to find the most efficient way to retrieve data.

Consider a SQL query that joins multiple tables to fetch data for a financial report. The query optimizer generates a query execution plan that outlines whether to use nested loops, hash joins, or other techniques to combine the data. Understanding and optimizing query execution plans is essential for efficient query performance.

Techniques for optimizing query execution plans include:

- **Index Hints:** Providing hints to the optimizer to influence its decisions.

- **Statistics Maintenance:** Ensuring that the database statistics are up to date.

- **Rewriting Queries:** Modifying queries to produce more efficient plans.

1.3.5. Hardware and Infrastructure

The underlying hardware and infrastructure on which the database runs have a significant impact on SQL performance. The choice of server hardware, storage devices, memory, and network configurations all influence database performance.

For example, using solid-state drives (SSDs) instead of traditional hard disk drives (HDDs) can significantly reduce disk latency and improve I/O performance. Similarly, adding more RAM to a database server can allow for larger in-memory caches, speeding up data retrieval.

Understanding the hardware constraints and opportunities is vital for optimizing SQL performance. Database administrators and system architects must collaborate to ensure that the infrastructure is aligned with performance goals.

1.3.6. Query Optimization Tools

Query optimization tools and utilities are invaluable assets in SQL performance tuning. These tools provide database administrators and developers with insights into query performance, query execution plans, and areas for improvement.

For example, SQL Profiler in Microsoft SQL Server allows users to trace and analyze query execution. Oracle Database provides tools like Oracle SQL Tuning Advisor for query optimization recommendations. These tools help identify performance bottlenecks and suggest optimizations.

Additionally, there are third-party tools and open-source solutions available for comprehensive SQL performance analysis and optimization.

1.3.7. Continuous Monitoring and Tuning

SQL performance tuning is not a one-time task; it's an ongoing process. Continuous monitoring of database performance, query execution times, and resource utilization is essential. By proactively identifying and addressing performance issues, organizations can ensure that their databases consistently deliver optimal performance.

Tools like database monitoring systems, log analyzers, and performance dashboards enable real-time monitoring. When performance deviations or bottlenecks are detected, administrators can take corrective actions

, such as optimizing queries, adding indexes, or adjusting server configurations.

1.3.8. Summary

In summary, SQL performance tuning involves a combination of optimizing SQL queries, designing efficient database schemas, utilizing indexing strategies, understanding query execution plans, considering hardware and infrastructure, leveraging query optimization tools, and continuously monitoring and tuning the database. These key components work together to ensure that a database system operates at peak performance, delivering a responsive user experience, cost savings, scalability, and a competitive advantage.

As we proceed through this guide, we will delve deeper into each of these components, providing practical insights, examples, and techniques to master the art of SQL performance tuning. Our journey begins with the SQL performance tuning process, which we explore in the next section.

PART II
Core Strategies for SQL Performance Tuning

2.1 The SQL Performance Tuning Process

In this section, we will dive deep into the SQL Performance Tuning Process, a systematic approach to enhancing the performance of your SQL queries and database systems. Understanding this process is essential for database administrators, developers, and anyone responsible for optimizing database performance.

2.1.1. Understanding the SQL Optimization Lifecycle

SQL optimization is not a one-time task but an ongoing process that follows a lifecycle. This lifecycle consists of several phases, each playing a crucial role in improving SQL query performance. Let's explore these phases in detail:

1. Identifying Performance Issues:

  - **The Trigger:** Performance tuning often begins when users complain about slow queries or when monitoring tools detect bottlenecks.

  - **Key Activities:**

    - **Gather User Feedback:** Talk to users to understand their pain points and gather specific examples of slow queries.

    - **Monitoring:** Use performance monitoring tools to identify resource-intensive queries and system bottlenecks.

  - **Outcome:** A list of performance issues that need attention.

2. Profiling and Analysis:

- **The Trigger:** Once issues are identified, it's essential to analyze and profile queries to pinpoint performance bottlenecks.

- **Key Activities:**

- **Query Profiling:** Use database-specific tools or profilers to capture query execution details.

- **Execution Plans:** Examine query execution plans to understand how the database engine processes queries.

- **Outcome:** A clear understanding of which parts of the query are consuming the most resources.

3. Setting Performance Goals and Metrics:

- **The Trigger:** Performance goals define what "good performance" means for your database system.

- **Key Activities:**

- **Define Objectives:** Determine what aspects of performance need improvement, such as query response times, throughput, or resource utilization.

- **Select Metrics:** Choose specific metrics (e.g., response time, throughput, resource usage) to measure improvements.

- **Establish Baselines:** Measure the current performance to establish a baseline for comparison.

- **Outcome:** Well-defined performance goals and metrics.

4. Query Optimization:

- **The Trigger:** Armed with performance goals, you can start optimizing queries.

- **Key Activities:**

- **Rewriting Queries:** Modify queries to use more efficient SQL constructs or reduce complexity.

- **Index Optimization:** Evaluate and create indexes to speed up query execution.

- **Parameterization:** Use parameterized queries to promote query plan reuse.

- **Outcome:** Optimized SQL queries that meet performance targets.

5. Testing and Validation:

- **The Trigger:** Before deploying changes to production, thoroughly test and validate the optimized queries.

- **Key Activities:**

- **Testing Environments:** Create testing environments that mimic production as closely as possible.

- **Benchmarking:** Use benchmark tests to measure query performance improvements.

- **Load Testing:** Assess query performance under various loads.

- **Outcome:** Confidence that the optimized queries will perform well in production.

6. Deployment and Monitoring:

- **The Trigger:** Once queries are optimized and validated, deploy them to the production environment.

- **Key Activities:**

- **Deployment Plan:** Develop a deployment plan that includes rollback procedures.

- **Continuous Monitoring:** Implement ongoing monitoring to detect and address any new performance issues.

- **Outcome:** Optimized queries in the production environment, with monitoring in place.

7. Continuous Improvement:

  - **The Trigger:** SQL performance tuning is an ongoing process.
  - **Key Activities:**
    - **Regular Review:** Continuously review query performance and address emerging issues.
    - **Feedback Loop:** Gather feedback from users and the operations team to refine your tuning efforts.
    - **Outcome:** A well-maintained and high-performing database system.

Example: SQL Optimization in an E-commerce Database

Let's illustrate these phases with an example from an e-commerce database:

Identifying Performance Issues: Users report slow product searches, and monitoring tools highlight spikes in CPU usage during peak shopping hours.

Profiling and Analysis: Profiling tools reveal that a complex search query is consuming most of the CPU resources. Execution plans show inefficient table scans.

Setting Performance Goals and Metrics: The goal is to reduce search query response times to under two seconds. Metrics include response time, CPU usage, and query throughput.

Query Optimization: The search query is rewritten to use optimized joins and filters. Indexes are created on frequently queried columns.

Testing and Validation: The optimized query is tested in a staging environment, subjected to benchmark and load tests, and consistently meets performance targets.

Deployment and Monitoring: The query is deployed to the production environment, and performance is continuously monitored to ensure it meets expectations.

Continuous Improvement: Regular reviews and user feedback lead to further optimization and adjustments based on changing usage patterns.

Understanding the SQL optimization lifecycle is fundamental to effective SQL performance tuning. It ensures that you systematically identify, address, and continuously improve the performance of your database systems and SQL queries.

2.1.2. Setting Performance Goals and Metrics

Setting clear and measurable performance goals is the cornerstone of any SQL performance tuning initiative. Without well-defined goals and metrics, it's challenging to assess whether your tuning efforts are successful. Let's break down the process of setting performance goals and metrics:

1. Define Objectives:

  - **Why Are You Tuning?:** Start by understanding the primary reason for SQL performance tuning. Is it to reduce query response times, enhance system throughput, or optimize resource utilization? Each objective may require different strategies.

  - **Prioritize Goals:** Identify which aspects of performance are most critical for your specific application. For example, an e-commerce site might prioritize quick product searches over generating sales reports.

2. Select Metrics:

- **Quantifiable Metrics:** Choose metrics that can be quantified, measured, and compared. Common SQL performance metrics include query response time, throughput (queries per second), CPU utilization, memory usage, and disk I/O.

- **Baseline Metrics:** To assess the impact of your tuning efforts, it's essential to establish baseline measurements. These are the metrics you collect before making any optimizations.

3. Establish Baselines:

- **Gather Current Metrics:** Use monitoring tools to collect baseline metrics from your existing system. This provides a starting point for comparison.

- **Capture Variability:** Understand that performance metrics can vary over time due to changes in user activity, data volume, or hardware capacity. Gather metrics during different load scenarios to capture this variability.

4. Define Targets:

- **Quantify Improvement:** Determine how much you want to improve each metric. For instance, you might aim to reduce query response times by 30% or increase throughput to support 100 queries per second.

- **Specific and Realistic:** Ensure your targets are specific and realistic. They should be achievable based on your current system's capabilities and constraints.

5. Create a Performance Measurement Plan:

- **What to Measure:** Specify which metrics you'll measure and how you'll collect them. Consider using monitoring tools, performance counters, or custom scripts.

- **Frequency:** Define how often you'll collect performance data. Real-time monitoring provides immediate insights, while periodic sampling is suitable for trend analysis.

- **Data Storage:** Determine where and how you'll store historical performance data. A database or dedicated storage solution can help you track long-term trends.

6. Develop Key Performance Indicators (KPIs):

- **KPIs:** Key Performance Indicators are specific metrics that directly align with your objectives. For example, if your goal is to improve the user experience, a KPI might be reducing the average page load time to under two seconds.

- **Monitor KPIs:** Keep a constant watch on your KPIs. When they meet your defined targets, you know your SQL performance tuning efforts have succeeded.

Example: Setting Performance Goals for an Inventory Management System

Let's consider an inventory management system used by a retail company as an example:

Define Objectives: The primary objective is to reduce the time it takes to generate inventory reports. Secondary objectives include improving the efficiency of order processing and ensuring real-time stock updates.

Select Metrics:

- **Query Response Time:** Measured in seconds, this metric indicates how quickly inventory reports are generated.

- **Throughput:** Measured in queries per second, it helps assess the system's ability to handle concurrent requests.

- **CPU and Memory Usage:** Monitoring these metrics ensures optimal resource utilization.

Establish Baselines: Collect baseline metrics during various times of the day, especially during peak shopping hours. This captures the system's performance under different loads.

Define Targets: The goal is to reduce the report generation time by 40%, increase throughput to handle 150 queries per second, and keep CPU utilization under 70%.

Create a Performance Measurement Plan: Implement real-time monitoring using performance monitoring tools to track query response times and resource usage. Collect data every five minutes and store it in a dedicated database.

Develop KPIs: The key performance indicator is achieving the 40% reduction in report generation time. Once this target is met and sustained, it signifies a successful performance tuning effort.

By following these steps and applying them to your specific SQL performance tuning project, you can set well-defined performance goals and metrics that act as guiding principles throughout the tuning process. These goals serve as benchmarks to measure the success of your optimizations and ensure that your efforts align with the desired outcomes.

2.1.3. Gathering Baseline Performance Data

Gathering baseline performance data involves capturing a snapshot of your database system's current state under typical operating conditions. This snapshot provides a clear understanding of the system's performance, identifies bottlenecks, and enables you to measure improvements accurately. Here's how to gather baseline performance data effectively:

1. Define Data Collection Scope:

 - **Identify Key Metrics:** Determine which performance metrics are relevant to your tuning objectives. Common metrics include CPU usage, memory utilization, disk I/O rates, and query response times.

- **Choose Monitoring Tools:** Select appropriate monitoring tools or utilities for collecting performance data. Most database management systems (DBMS) offer built-in monitoring features, and there are also third-party tools available.

- **Establish a Collection Frequency:** Decide how frequently you'll collect performance data. Real-time monitoring provides continuous insights, while periodic snapshots are suitable for trend analysis.

2. Prepare a Baseline Environment:

- **Stable Conditions:** Ensure that your database environment is under stable and typical load conditions during data collection. Avoid performing data-intensive operations or running unusual workloads.

- **Data Sampling:** For long-term trend analysis, it's essential to capture data over an extended period. Consider collecting data over several days or weeks.

3. Capture Key Metrics:

- **Resource Utilization:** Monitor resource utilization metrics such as CPU usage, memory consumption, disk I/O rates, and network traffic. These metrics help identify resource bottlenecks.

- **Query Performance:** Analyze query response times and execution plans. Identify slow-running queries, query frequency, and the most resource-intensive queries.

- **Database Metrics:** Examine database-specific metrics like the number of connections, transaction rates, and buffer pool hit ratios.

4. Data Storage and Retention:

- **Data Repository:** Designate a storage location for your performance data. It can be a database, a dedicated server, or a cloud-based storage solution.

- **Data Retention Policy:** Define how long you'll retain baseline data. Long-term retention allows for historical analysis and trend identification.

5. Automated Monitoring:

- **Alerts and Thresholds:** Configure automated alerts based on predefined thresholds. These alerts notify you of performance anomalies or critical issues in real-time.

- **Scheduled Reports:** Implement automated reporting to generate periodic summaries of performance data. Scheduled reports help keep stakeholders informed.

6. Documentation:

- **Record Configurations:** Maintain documentation of your system's configurations, including hardware specifications, software versions, and database settings.

- **Annotations:** Annotate your performance data with relevant contextual information. This includes any changes made to the system or queries during the data collection period.

7. Analyze and Interpret Data:

- **Comparative Analysis:** After gathering baseline data, perform a comparative analysis to identify deviations from typical behavior. Look for patterns or trends that may indicate performance issues.

- **Identify Bottlenecks:** Pinpoint bottlenecks or limitations in your current system based on the collected metrics. For instance, if CPU usage consistently reaches 90%, it could be a CPU bottleneck.

- **Query Optimization Targets:** Review query performance data to identify queries that require optimization. Queries with high execution times or frequent resource utilization are prime candidates.

8. Establish Performance Metrics Thresholds:

- **Threshold Definitions:** Define performance thresholds that indicate when a metric is in an acceptable or problematic state. Thresholds vary based on your system's requirements and performance goals.

- **Actionable Thresholds:** Ensure that thresholds are actionable, meaning they trigger specific actions when crossed. For example, a high query error rate could trigger an alert for immediate investigation.

9. Monitor and Review:

- **Continuous Monitoring:** Implement continuous monitoring to track performance over time. Regularly review performance data to identify emerging issues or trends.

- **Periodic Baseline Updates:** As your system evolves, periodically update your baseline performance data to reflect changes in usage patterns or configurations.

Example: Gathering Baseline Performance Data

Consider a scenario where you're responsible for tuning the performance of an e-commerce website's database:

Define Data Collection Scope:

- **Key Metrics:** You decide to monitor CPU usage, memory consumption, disk I/O rates, and the response time of critical queries.

- **Monitoring Tools:** You choose to use the built-in performance monitoring features of your database management system.

- **Collection Frequency:** You set up real-time monitoring for CPU and memory usage and collect query performance data every 15 minutes.

Prepare a Baseline Environment:

- **Stable Conditions:** You ensure that the website is operating under typical conditions, without any major promotions or unusual traffic spikes.

- **Data Sampling:** To capture long-term trends, you plan to collect data continuously for a month.

Capture Key Metrics:

- **Resource Utilization:** You monitor

CPU usage, memory utilization, disk I/O rates, and network traffic.

- **Query Performance:** You track the response times of key database queries, their execution plans, and query frequency.

Data Storage and Retention:

- **Data Repository:** You store performance data in a dedicated database on the same server.

- **Data Retention Policy:** You decide to retain data for six months to allow for historical analysis.

Automated Monitoring:

- **Alerts and Thresholds:** You set up alerts to trigger when CPU usage exceeds 90% for more than 10 minutes.

- **Scheduled Reports:** Automated reports summarizing weekly performance data are sent to relevant stakeholders.

Documentation:

- Record Configurations: You maintain records of server hardware specifications, software versions, and database settings.

- Annotations: You add annotations to the performance data, noting any system changes or query optimizations made during the data collection period.

Analyzing and Interpreting Data:

- Comparative Analysis: You compare current performance metrics to historical data and identify a gradual increase in query response times.

- Identify Bottlenecks: Based on CPU and memory usage, you identify that CPU resources are a potential bottleneck.

- Query Optimization Targets: Query performance data reveals a specific query that consistently consumes a high amount of CPU and has a slow response time.

Establish Performance Metrics Thresholds:

- Threshold Definitions: You define a threshold for CPU usage where 90% or higher triggers an alert.

- Actionable Thresholds: When the CPU usage exceeds the threshold, an automated alert is sent to the on-call DBA team for investigation.

Monitor and Review:

- Continuous Monitoring: You implement continuous monitoring to detect performance anomalies promptly.

- Periodic Baseline Updates: You plan to update your baseline performance data quarterly to account for seasonal traffic variations.

By following these steps, you can effectively gather baseline performance data for your SQL database system, providing a solid foundation for subsequent performance tuning efforts. This data empowers you to make informed decisions, prioritize optimizations, and measure the impact of changes accurately.

2.2 Investigating Issues: Identifying Performance Bottlenecks

In the realm of SQL performance tuning, identifying and addressing performance bottlenecks is akin to diagnosing an ailment in a patient before prescribing the cure. This crucial phase involves a deep dive into the database system to uncover the root causes of performance degradation. Let's explore the steps to identify common performance bottlenecks effectively.

2.2.1. Identifying Common Performance Bottlenecks

Performance bottlenecks are specific points in a database system where resources or processes are constrained, leading to reduced overall performance. Common bottlenecks include CPU limitations, memory shortages, slow disk I/O, and poorly optimized queries. Here's a systematic approach to identifying these bottlenecks:

1. Monitoring Resource Utilization:

 - **CPU Utilization:** Start by monitoring CPU usage. High and sustained CPU utilization can indicate a CPU bottleneck. Use operating system utilities or database management system (DBMS) tools to track CPU metrics.

 - **Memory Consumption:** Examine memory usage patterns. If available memory is consistently exhausted, it may lead to paging or swapping, degrading performance. Review both physical and virtual memory usage.

 - **Disk I/O Rates:** Analyze disk I/O rates, including read and write operations. High disk I/O, particularly for random reads or writes, can suggest disk bottlenecks.

 - **Network Activity:** For distributed systems, keep an eye on network activity. Network saturation or high latency can impact performance.

2. Database Query Analysis:

- **Query Response Times:** Identify queries with slow response times. Slow-running queries are often a source of performance bottlenecks. Database profiling tools or DBMS-specific query monitoring features can help.

- **Execution Plans:** Review query execution plans to ensure they are optimized. Suboptimal execution plans can lead to increased resource consumption.

- **Query Frequency:** Analyze query frequency. Queries executed too frequently can overload the system, especially if they are resource-intensive.

3. Locking and Blocking Analysis:

- **Lock Waits:** Investigate lock waits and blocking issues. Lock contention can lead to query delays and reduced concurrency.

- **Deadlocks:** Look for deadlock occurrences. Deadlocks can bring transactions to a standstill and require manual intervention.

4. Resource Pooling and Connection Management:

- **Connection Pooling:** Evaluate the use of connection pooling mechanisms. Connection pool mismanagement can lead to excessive resource consumption and contention.

- **Connection Leaks:** Check for connection leaks where connections are not properly closed after use. Connection leaks can deplete available resources over time.

5. Disk I/O Performance:

- **Disk Health:** Assess the health of storage devices. Failing or degraded disks can significantly impact I/O performance.

- **Storage Configuration:** Review storage configuration, including RAID levels and disk partitioning. Suboptimal configurations can lead to I/O bottlenecks.

6. Database Logs and Monitoring:

- **Transaction Logs:** Inspect transaction logs for any anomalies. High transaction log activity can affect performance.

- **Database Monitoring:** Utilize database monitoring tools to gain insights into system behavior and resource consumption.

7. Profiling and Profilers:

- **Profiling Tools:** Consider using profiling tools or performance monitoring solutions. Profilers can capture detailed data on query execution, resource usage, and system behavior.

8. Systematic Testing:

- **Load Testing:** Perform load testing to simulate high loads and stress conditions. Observe how the system behaves under stress and identify points of failure.

- **Scenario-Based Testing:** Create testing scenarios that mimic real-world usage patterns. This can reveal performance issues specific to certain user interactions or workflows.

Example: Identifying a CPU Bottleneck

Suppose you observe consistently high CPU utilization on your database server during peak hours, resulting in sluggish query response times. To identify and address this performance bottleneck:

1. Monitoring Resource Utilization:
- Use an operating system monitoring tool to track CPU usage over time.

- Identify periods of sustained high CPU utilization.

2. Database Query Analysis:

   - Analyze slow-running queries using a query performance analysis tool.

   - Examine query execution plans to ensure they are optimized.

3. Locking and Blocking Analysis:

   - Investigate lock waits and deadlocks using database logs and monitoring tools.

4. Resource Pooling and Connection Management:

   - Review the connection pool configuration to ensure it is appropriately sized.

   - Check for connection leaks in the application code.

5. Disk I/O Performance:

   - Check the health of storage devices and RAID configurations.

   - Review the partitioning scheme to ensure balanced I/O distribution.

6. Database Logs and Monitoring:

   - Inspect transaction logs for any irregularities.

   - Use a database monitoring tool to gather additional insights.

By systematically addressing each of these areas, you can pinpoint the CPU bottleneck's root cause and implement targeted solutions to alleviate the performance issue.

Best Practices for Identifying Bottlenecks:

1. Regularly monitor and analyze resource utilization.

2. Implement proactive monitoring and alerting for critical resources.

3. Use profiling and monitoring tools to gain deeper insights.

4. Collaborate with developers to review and optimize queries.

5. Continuously update your knowledge of database performance tuning techniques.

Identifying common performance bottlenecks is a crucial step in the SQL performance tuning process. Once identified, these bottlenecks can be addressed, leading to significant improvements in database system performance.

2.2.2. Using Profiling and Monitoring Tools

In the quest for optimal SQL performance, identifying and addressing performance bottlenecks is paramount. In the digital age, where databases handle vast amounts of data and complex queries, performance bottlenecks can lurk in various corners of your database system. This section delves into the practical aspects of using profiling and monitoring tools to pinpoint these bottlenecks and lays out a step-by-step guide to help you through the process.

Why Identifying Performance Bottlenecks Is Crucial

Performance bottlenecks are points within your database system where performance slows down or becomes constrained, adversely affecting the user experience. Identifying them is crucial for several reasons:

1. Optimization Focus: Knowing where the bottlenecks are allows you to focus your optimization efforts precisely, rather than making blanket changes that may not yield the desired results.

2. Resource Allocation: You can allocate resources efficiently. For instance, if you identify that CPU usage is a bottleneck, you can consider scaling up your CPU resources or optimizing resource-hungry queries.

3. User Satisfaction: Addressing bottlenecks directly impacts user satisfaction. Faster response times and smoother interactions lead to happier users.

4. Cost Savings: Optimizing specific bottlenecks can result in cost savings. For example, reducing excessive disk I/O can lower infrastructure costs.

Step-by-Step Guide: Using Profiling and Monitoring Tools to Identify Bottlenecks

Here's a comprehensive guide on how to use profiling and monitoring tools to identify performance bottlenecks in your SQL database system:

Step 1: Tool Selection

  - Choose a profiling and monitoring tool compatible with your database system. For instance, if you're using Microsoft SQL Server, SQL Server Profiler is a dedicated tool for this purpose.

Step 2: Installation and Configuration

  - Install the selected tool on a dedicated server or workstation that has access to the database server.

  - Configure the tool to connect to your database server. Provide the necessary credentials and connection details.

Step 3: Define Performance Metrics

- Determine which performance metrics are critical for your analysis. These may include CPU usage, memory consumption, disk I/O rates, query execution times, lock wait times, and more.

- Configure the profiling tool to capture and display these metrics.

Step 4: Set Thresholds and Alerts

- Establish threshold values for each monitored metric. These thresholds should indicate acceptable performance ranges.

- Configure alerting rules within the monitoring tool to trigger notifications when predefined thresholds are breached. Alerts can be sent via email, SMS, or integrated with alert management systems.

Step 5: Real-Time Monitoring

- Start the monitoring process and observe real-time data. The tool will continuously collect and display performance metrics.

- Keep an eye on performance dashboards, graphs, and tables to detect any abnormalities.

Step 6: Query Analysis

- Utilize the profiling tool's query analysis features to identify slow-running queries and resource-intensive operations.

- Examine query execution plans, query statistics, and resource consumption data to pinpoint optimization opportunities.

Step 7: Troubleshooting

- When performance issues arise or bottlenecks are detected, use the gathered data to diagnose the root causes.

- Take corrective actions, which may include query optimization, index adjustments, or resource allocation changes.

Step 8: Historical Data Analysis

- Leverage historical data stored by the profiling and monitoring tool to analyze long-term trends and performance patterns.

- Historical data analysis can guide capacity planning and proactive optimizations.

Step 9: Regular Review

- Schedule regular reviews of the monitoring data to ensure ongoing performance optimization.

- Adjust monitoring thresholds and alerts as needed based on evolving system requirements.

Example: Identifying a Disk I/O Bottleneck

Let's illustrate this process with an example of identifying and addressing a common performance bottleneck: excessive disk I/O. This issue can significantly impact database performance, especially when queries frequently read or write data to disk.

1. Select a Profiling Tool: In this scenario, we're using SQL Server Profiler for a Microsoft SQL Server database.

2. Configuration: Install SQL Server Profiler on a workstation with access to the SQL Server instance. Configure it to connect to the target database and select relevant events to monitor, such as "Batch Starting" and "Batch Completed."

3. Monitor in Real-Time: Start the trace and let it run while the application generates typical database activity. Monitor real-time data through the profiler's interface.

4. Analyze Disk I/O Metrics: Pay close attention to disk I/O-related metrics, such as "Reads," "Writes," and "Disk Latency." If you notice high values or spikes in these metrics, it indicates potential disk I/O bottlenecks.

5. Identify Problematic Queries: Use the profiler's query analysis features to identify the SQL queries responsible for the excessive disk I/O. You can examine the execution plans and statistics for these queries.

6. Optimization Steps: Once you've identified the problematic queries, work on optimizing them. This may involve index optimization, query rewriting, or reducing unnecessary data reads and writes.

7. Monitor and Verify: After implementing optimizations, continue monitoring disk I/O metrics to ensure the bottleneck has been alleviated. You should observe a decrease in disk activity for the previously problematic queries.

By following this process, you can successfully identify and address a disk I/O bottleneck using profiling and monitoring tools. Similar steps can be applied to other types of bottlenecks, such as CPU or memory constraints.

Conclusion

Identifying and addressing performance bottlenecks is a critical aspect of SQL performance tuning. Profiling and monitoring tools provide the means to achieve this effectively. By selecting the right tools, configuring them correctly, and following a systematic approach to monitoring and analysis, you can pinpoint bottlenecks, diagnose root causes, and implement optimizations that significantly enhance your SQL database system's performance.

2.2.3. Analyzing Query Execution Plans

Analyzing query execution plans is a fundamental skill in the quest for SQL performance optimization. A query execution plan, also known as a query plan or execution plan, is a detailed blueprint that the database management system (DBMS) uses to execute a SQL query efficiently. In this section, we will explore why query execution plans matter, how to access them, and how to interpret them effectively to identify and resolve performance bottlenecks.

Why Query Execution Plans Matter

Query execution plans are crucial for several reasons:

1. Performance Insights: They provide insights into how the DBMS processes your SQL queries. This includes the order in which tables are accessed, the types of joins performed, and the indexes used.

2. Bottleneck Identification: Query plans highlight potential bottlenecks, such as full table scans, inefficient join operations, or excessive sorting. By examining these aspects, you can identify performance issues.

3. Optimization Guidance: They offer guidance for query optimization. You can see whether indexes are being utilized, and if not, you can consider adding or modifying them to improve query performance.

4. Debugging: When a query is not returning the expected results or is running slowly, the query plan can help you understand why. It's a valuable tool for debugging SQL queries.

Accessing Query Execution Plans

Most modern database systems offer tools and commands to access query execution plans. Here are common methods for accessing query plans:

1. Using SQL Profilers: Profiling tools like SQL Server Profiler, Oracle Trace, and MySQL Performance Schema capture query execution plans as part of their monitoring capabilities.

2. EXPLAIN Statement: Many database systems, including MySQL, PostgreSQL, and SQLite, support an `EXPLAIN` statement. By prefixing your SQL query with `EXPLAIN`, you can retrieve the query plan.

3. Database Management Studio (DBMS): Integrated development environments (IDEs) or DBMS-specific tools often provide graphical interfaces to view query execution plans. For example, SQL Server Management Studio (SSMS) has a built-in query plan viewer.

4. Command-Line Utilities: Some databases offer command-line utilities for accessing query plans. For instance, PostgreSQL provides the `pg_query_plan` utility.

Interpreting Query Execution Plans

Analyzing query execution plans can be intricate, but a step-by-step approach simplifies the process. Let's break down how to interpret query plans effectively:

Step 1: Retrieve the Query Plan

   - Use one of the methods mentioned earlier to retrieve the query execution plan for your SQL query.

Step 2: Understand the Nodes

- Query plans are often represented as trees or diagrams. Each node in the tree corresponds to an operation performed during query execution.

- Common nodes include "Scan," "Seek," "Join," "Sort," and "Aggregate."

Step 3: Node Details

- For each node, review the details provided. This typically includes information about the table or index being accessed, the number of rows, and any predicates applied.

- Look for nodes with high resource utilization or large row counts, as these can indicate performance bottlenecks.

Step 4: Table and Index Access

- Check if indexes are used as intended. Look for "Index Seek" or "Index Scan" nodes, which indicate index usage. If you see "Table Scan," it implies a full table scan, which is less efficient.

Step 5: Joins and Sorting

- Examine join operations. Ensure that the join order is optimal and that indexes are used for joining whenever possible.

- Identify any sorting operations. Sorting large result sets can impact performance.

Step 6: Filtering and Predicates

- Evaluate any filtering conditions (e.g., `WHERE` clauses). Ensure that indexes support these conditions to reduce the number of rows processed.

Step 7: Cost Estimations

- Some query plans include cost estimations. While these values can be useful, they are not always precise. Use them as rough indicators rather than absolute values.

Step 8: Plan Changes

- Consider modifying the query or indexes based on your analysis. If you identify bottlenecks or inefficiencies, optimizing the query plan can lead to significant performance improvements.

Example: Analyzing a Query Execution Plan

Let's consider an example using SQL Server Management Studio (SSMS) to analyze a query execution plan:

1. Retrieve the Plan: In SSMS, execute the query with the "Include Actual Execution Plan" option enabled (Ctrl+M). This displays the execution plan alongside the query results.

2. Review the Plan: Examine the query plan, starting from the top (rightmost) node. Each node represents an operation in the query.

3. Node Details: Click on nodes to view details

. Look for table or index access methods, join types, and any expensive operations.

4. Identify Issues: Identify potential bottlenecks or areas for optimization. For example, a "Table Scan" on a large table might indicate a need for indexing.

5. Optimize: Based on your analysis, consider optimizing the query, adding indexes, or modifying the SQL statement to improve performance.

By following these steps and gaining proficiency in analyzing query execution plans, you can effectively identify and resolve performance bottlenecks in your SQL queries, ultimately enhancing the overall performance of your database system.

2.3 Optimizing Existing SQL Statements

2.3.1. Identifying Problematic SQL Statements

Identifying problematic SQL statements is the crucial first step in optimizing your database's performance. These statements are often the root cause of performance bottlenecks. In this section, we will delve into techniques and best practices for identifying such statements.

Why Identify Problematic SQL Statements?

Problematic SQL statements can significantly impact your application's performance, leading to slow response times and increased resource utilization. Identifying these statements is essential for several reasons:

1. Targeted Optimization: By pinpointing problematic queries, you can focus your optimization efforts where they will have the most significant impact.

2. Resource Efficiency: Optimization consumes time and resources. Identifying problematic statements ensures you allocate these resources wisely.

3. Improved User Experience: Resolving performance issues in critical queries enhances the user experience and reduces frustration.

4. Capacity Planning: Identifying resource-intensive queries helps in capacity planning and hardware scaling decisions.

Here's a step-by-step guide on how to identify problematic SQL statements:

Step 1: Gather Performance Metrics

Begin by collecting performance metrics from your database system. Common metrics include query execution times, CPU and memory usage, and disk I/O. Most database management systems offer tools for monitoring these metrics. Third-party monitoring tools can also be valuable.

Step 2: Review Long-Running Queries

Identify queries that have long execution times. Long-running queries are prime candidates for optimization. Check your performance metrics for queries that consistently rank high in terms of execution duration.

Step 3: Monitor Blocking and Deadlocks

Blocking and deadlocks can significantly impact query performance. Utilize database monitoring tools to detect and analyze these issues. Queries involved in blocking or deadlocks may require optimization.

Step 4: Analyze Query Execution Plans

Database management systems provide tools for examining query execution plans. Review these plans to identify inefficient queries. Pay attention to areas where full table scans or large joins occur, as these can indicate optimization opportunities.

Step 5: Utilize Query Profilers

Query profiling tools capture detailed information about query execution, such as the number of rows processed and the time spent in various stages of query execution. Profilers can help you identify bottlenecks within queries.

Step 6: Review Database Logs

Database logs often contain information about queries that are generating errors or warnings. Analyze these logs to identify queries that require attention.

Step 7: Implement Monitoring Alerts

Set up monitoring alerts to notify you when certain performance thresholds are breached. For example, you can create alerts for queries that exceed a predefined execution time or consume excessive system resources.

Step 8: Leverage Database Management System Features

Many database systems offer built-in features for identifying problematic queries. For example, SQL Server has the Query Store, which tracks query performance over time and highlights regressions.

Common Indicators of Problematic Queries

While monitoring and analyzing your database's performance, keep an eye out for the following indicators that may signal problematic queries:

1. High CPU or Memory Usage: Queries that consume a disproportionate amount of CPU or memory resources are candidates for optimization.

2. Long Execution Times: Queries with long execution times, especially if they are part of critical operations, should be optimized to reduce latency.

3. Full Table Scans: Queries that perform full table scans rather than using available indexes can be optimized by adding or modifying indexes.

4. High Disk I/O: Queries causing high disk I/O can benefit from optimizations to reduce data retrieval and storage operations.

5. Blocking or Deadlocks: Queries involved in blocking or deadlock situations require attention to improve concurrency.

Practical Example: Identifying a Problematic Query

Let's walk through an example of identifying a problematic query and understanding why it needs optimization:

Consider the following query:

```sql
SELECT *
FROM orders
WHERE order_status = 'Pending'
```

This query retrieves all pending orders. Upon analyzing performance metrics, you notice that this query takes longer to execute as the number of orders in the database increases. It's a prime candidate for optimization.

Key observations:

- The query lacks an index on the `order_status` column, leading to a full table scan.

- It retrieves all columns, which may be unnecessary if only specific data is needed.

To optimize this query, you can:

- Add an index on the `order_status` column to improve filtering efficiency.

- Select only the necessary columns instead of using `SELECT *` to reduce data retrieval overhead.

By following these optimization steps, you can transform a problematic query into a more efficient one, improving overall database performance.

In conclusion, identifying problematic SQL statements is the foundation of effective performance tuning. By diligently monitoring and analyzing performance metrics, query execution plans, and common indicators of performance issues, you can pinpoint queries that require optimization and take targeted actions to enhance your database's efficiency.

2.3.2. Rewriting Queries for Improved Performance

Rewriting SQL queries is a fundamental technique in SQL performance tuning. It involves modifying the structure and logic of existing queries to make them more efficient and improve overall database performance. In this section, we will explore the reasons for query rewriting, common rewriting strategies, and practical examples of query optimization.

Why Rewrite Queries for Improved Performance?

SQL query optimization often begins with rewriting queries, and for good reasons:

1. Inefficient Logic: Over time, as databases evolve, SQL queries may become less efficient due to changes in data volume or data distribution. Rewriting allows you to adapt queries to new requirements.

2. Suboptimal Execution Plans: The database query optimizer may not always generate the best execution plan. Query rewriting can help guide the optimizer to choose a more efficient plan.

3. Complex Queries: As applications grow, queries can become complex with multiple joins, subqueries, and conditional logic. Rewriting can simplify queries without sacrificing functionality.

4. Parameterization: Rewriting can involve parameterizing queries, making them adaptable to various input values and promoting query plan reuse.

5. Compatibility: Query rewriting can ensure that queries are compatible with different database systems or versions, making code more portable.

Now, let's dive into the process of rewriting SQL queries for improved performance:

Step 1: Identify Problematic Queries

Before you can begin rewriting queries, you need to identify which queries are problematic. This can be done through query profiling, monitoring, and analyzing performance metrics, as discussed in previous sections.

Step 2: Review Query Execution Plans

For each identified problematic query, review its query execution plan. Understanding how the database processes the query can reveal opportunities for optimization.

Step 3: Simplify WHERE Clauses

One common query optimization technique is to simplify WHERE clauses. This involves:

- **Removing Redundant Conditions:** Identify and eliminate conditions that are always true or always false. For example, `WHERE 1=1` is always true and can be removed.

- **Avoiding Complex Expressions:** Replace complex expressions in WHERE clauses with simpler ones. For example, consider using `BETWEEN` instead of a combination of `>=` and `<=` operators.

Step 4: Optimize Joins

If your query involves multiple tables and joins, optimizing join operations can significantly improve performance. Consider the following strategies:

- Use INNER JOIN: Whenever possible, use INNER JOIN instead of OUTER JOIN. INNER JOIN returns only matching rows and tends to be faster.

- Reduce the Number of Joins: Minimize the number of tables involved in a query. Excessive joins can lead to performance degradation.

- Consider Indexes: Ensure that columns involved in join conditions are indexed for faster lookup.

Step 5: Rewrite Subqueries

Subqueries can be performance bottlenecks, especially when used in the SELECT or WHERE clauses. Consider these subquery optimization techniques:

- Convert to JOINs: Subqueries can often be rewritten as JOIN operations, which are generally more efficient.

- Aggregate Functions: Replace correlated subqueries that use aggregate functions with JOINs and GROUP BY clauses.

Step 6: Parameterization

Parameterizing queries involves using parameters instead of hardcoding values directly into SQL statements. This promotes query plan reuse and adaptability. Most database systems support parameterized queries using placeholders, such as `?` or `:param`.

Step 7: Test and Benchmark

After rewriting queries, it's essential to test and benchmark their performance. Compare the execution times and resource utilization before and after the rewrite. Ensure that the rewritten query returns correct results.

Practical Examples

Let's explore some practical examples of query rewriting for improved performance:

Example 1: Redundant WHERE Clause

Consider the following query:

```sql
SELECT * FROM products WHERE 1=1 AND category = 'Electronics';
```

This query has a redundant condition `1=1`, which doesn't affect the result set. You can rewrite it as:

```sql
SELECT * FROM products WHERE category = 'Electronics';
```

Example 2: Complex JOIN Condition

Suppose you have a query with a complex JOIN condition like this:

```sql
SELECT * FROM orders
JOIN customers ON
  orders.customer_id = customers.id AND
  orders.order_date >= '2023-01-01';
```

You can simplify the condition and move the date filter to the WHERE clause:

```sql
SELECT * FROM orders
JOIN customers ON orders.customer_id = customers.id
WHERE orders.order_date >= '2023-01-01';
```

Example 3: Subquery Optimization

Consider a query with a subquery in the SELECT clause:

```sql
SELECT customer_name, (SELECT COUNT(*) FROM orders WHERE orders.customer_id =
customers.id) AS order_count
FROM customers;
```

```
```
You can rewrite this query using a JOIN and GROUP BY for better performance:

```sql
SELECT customers.customer_name, COUNT(orders.id) AS order_count
FROM customers
LEFT JOIN orders ON customers.id = orders.customer_id
GROUP BY customers.customer_name;
```

These examples demonstrate how query rewriting can simplify complex queries and lead to improved performance. By identifying and addressing inefficiencies in your SQL statements, you can enhance the overall performance of your database system.

2.3.3. Implementing Parameterization

Parameterization is a critical technique in optimizing SQL statements, particularly those that are frequently executed with different parameter values. By implementing parameterization, you can improve query reuse, reduce query compilation overhead, and enhance overall database performance. In this section, we will explore the concept of parameterization, why it matters, and how to implement it effectively.

Why Implement Parameterization?

Parameterization is essential for several reasons:

1. Query Reuse: Parameterized queries allow the database management system (DBMS) to reuse query execution plans. This reduces the need for repeated query compilation, leading to faster query execution.

2. Security: Parameterization helps prevent SQL injection attacks by separating SQL code from parameter values. It ensures that user inputs are treated as data rather than executable code.

3. Maintainability: Parameterized queries are more maintainable and readable. They separate SQL logic from parameter values, making the code easier to understand and modify.

4. Improved Performance: By eliminating the need to recompile queries with different parameter values, parameterization reduces CPU and memory overhead, resulting in improved performance.

Types of Parameterization

There are two primary types of parameterization: implicit and explicit.

Implicit Parameterization:

Implicit parameterization, also known as simple parameterization, is the automatic conversion of literal values in SQL statements into parameters. The DBMS recognizes queries with literal values and converts them into parameterized queries during query compilation. This process is typically transparent to developers.

Here's an example of implicit parameterization:

```sql
```

```
-- Original SQL statement with literals

SELECT * FROM employees WHERE employee_id = 101;


-- Implicitly parameterized query

SELECT * FROM employees WHERE employee_id = @p1;
```

In this example, the DBMS implicitly converts the literal value `101` into a parameter named `@p1`.

Explicit Parameterization:

Explicit parameterization, as the name suggests, involves developers explicitly defining parameters in their SQL statements. Developers specify parameter names and data types, making it a more controlled and intentional process.

Here's an example of explicit parameterization:


```sql
-- Explicitly parameterized query

SELECT * FROM employees WHERE employee_id = @employee_id;
```


In this example, the developer explicitly defines the `@employee_id` parameter.

Benefits of Explicit Parameterization:

While implicit parameterization is convenient and requires minimal developer intervention, explicit parameterization offers more control and some distinct advantages:

1. Improved Query Plan Reuse: With explicit parameterization, developers can ensure consistent parameter names and data types across queries, increasing query plan reuse.

2. Enhanced Readability: Explicit parameters make SQL statements more readable and self-documenting, improving code maintainability.

3. Reduced Risk of Errors: Explicit parameterization reduces the risk of accidental SQL injection vulnerabilities by clearly separating SQL logic from parameter values.

Implementing Parameterization

Implementing parameterization involves converting SQL statements with literal values into parameterized queries. The exact steps vary depending on your database system and programming language. Below, we'll outline the general process for implementing parameterization:

Step 1: Identify SQL Statements to Parameterize

Start by identifying SQL statements in your application that would benefit from parameterization. Focus on queries with frequently changing parameter values or those susceptible to SQL injection.

Step 2: Choose the Appropriate Parameterization Method

Decide whether to use implicit or explicit parameterization based on your application's requirements and coding practices. While implicit parameterization may be suitable for simple cases, explicit parameterization provides more control and is recommended for complex queries.

Step 3: Replace Literal Values with Parameters

For implicit parameterization, you may not need to take any action, as the DBMS will handle it automatically. However, for explicit parameterization, replace literal values in your SQL statements with parameter placeholders. Parameter placeholders are typically represented by a symbol or a name, depending on your DBMS.

```sql
-- Original SQL statement with literals
SELECT * FROM employees WHERE employee_id = 101;

-- Explicitly parameterized query
SELECT * FROM employees WHERE employee_id = @employee_id;
```

In this example, we've replaced the literal `101` with the parameter `@employee_id`.

Step 4: Define Parameters in Your Code

In your application code, define the parameters you've used in your SQL statements. Assign appropriate values to these parameters before executing the queries.

The exact syntax for defining parameters and assigning values depends on your programming language and database library. Below is an example in C# using ADO.NET:

```
using System.Data.SqlClient;

// Define a connection and SQL command
using (SqlConnection connection = new SqlConnection(connectionString))
{
    connection.Open();

    // Define the SQL command with parameters
    string sql = "SELECT * FROM employees WHERE employee_id = @employee_id";
    SqlCommand command = new SqlCommand(sql, connection);

    // Define and assign values to parameters
    command.Parameters.AddWithValue("@employee_id", 101);

    // Execute the query
    SqlDataReader reader = command.ExecuteReader();

    // Process query results
    // ...
}
```

Step 5: Test and Validate

Thoroughly test your parameterized queries with various parameter values to ensure they work correctly. Pay attention to edge cases and potential SQL injection scenarios.

Step 6: Monitor and Optimize

Even after parameterization, it's essential to monitor query performance. Use database profiling and monitoring tools to identify any further optimization opportunities. Query execution plans, indexing, and database design can still impact performance.

Conclusion

Parameterization is a fundamental technique in SQL performance tuning. It improves query reuse, enhances security, and contributes to code maintainability. Whether you opt for implicit or explicit parameterization, the goal is to separate SQL logic from parameter values, reducing overhead and improving the overall performance of your database-driven applications.

2.4 Optimizing SQL Statements for Enhanced Performance

2.4.1. Utilizing Indexes Effectively

Indexing is a crucial aspect of SQL performance tuning. When used effectively, indexes can significantly enhance the speed of query execution. However, improper or excessive use of indexes can lead to performance degradation. In this section, we will delve into the world of database indexing, exploring how to utilize indexes effectively to boost SQL statement performance.

Understanding Database Indexing

At its core, an index is a data structure that provides a quick way to look up data in a table. Think of it as a book's index, which allows you to find specific topics without reading the entire book. In the context of a database, an index helps the database management system (DBMS) quickly locate rows in a table based on the values in one or more columns.

Let's break down the key components of indexing:

- **Indexed Columns:** These are the columns on which the index is created. Queries often filter or sort data based on these columns.

- **Index Key:** An index key is a sorted list of values from the indexed column(s). The key is stored separately from the actual data, allowing for efficient lookups.

- **Pointer to Data:** The index contains pointers or references to the corresponding rows in the table where the data is stored.

Why Indexing Matters

Indexing plays a critical role in SQL performance because it:

1. Speeds Up Data Retrieval: Without indexes, the DBMS would need to scan the entire table to locate specific rows, which can be extremely slow for large datasets. Indexes enable the DBMS to quickly narrow down the search.

2. Reduces Disk I/O: Efficient indexes minimize the amount of disk I/O required for queries. This is crucial for overall system performance and resource optimization.

3. Enhances Query Performance: Queries with indexed columns can benefit from significant performance improvements. Simple SELECT, JOIN, and WHERE clauses can execute much faster with the right indexes.

Choosing the Right Columns to Index

Effective indexing starts with selecting the appropriate columns to index. Not every column in a table needs an index. Here are some considerations for choosing which columns to index:

1. Columns Used in WHERE Clauses: Index columns that are frequently used in WHERE clauses, especially those involved in equality comparisons (e.g., `WHERE username = 'John'`). These indexes are known as equality indexes.

2. Columns Used in JOINs: If you frequently join tables on specific columns, consider indexing those columns. These are known as join indexes.

3. Columns Used for Sorting: If you often sort query results based on a particular column (e.g., `ORDER BY creation_date`), consider creating an index on that column.

4. Columns with High Cardinality: Columns with high cardinality (many distinct values) tend to benefit from indexing. For example, a column containing unique user IDs is a good candidate for indexing.

5. Avoid Over-Indexing: While indexes can improve query performance, over-indexing can lead to maintenance overhead and potential performance degradation during data modifications (INSERT, UPDATE, DELETE operations). Strike a balance between query performance and data modification efficiency.

Types of Indexes

There are various types of indexes, each suited for different scenarios:

1. B-Tree Indexes: These are the most common type of indexes, suitable for equality and range queries. They organize data in a balanced tree structure for efficient lookups.

2. Hash Indexes: Ideal for equality comparisons but not for range queries or sorting. Hash indexes work well with columns that have a low cardinality.

3. Bitmap Indexes: These indexes are efficient for columns with a small number of distinct values. They use bitmaps to represent whether a value exists or not.

4. Full-Text Indexes: Designed for searching within text data, full-text indexes enable efficient text-based searches.

5. Spatial Indexes: Used for geographic or spatial data, these indexes optimize location-based queries.

6. Composite Indexes: Also known as multi-column indexes, these include more than one column in the index key. They are useful when queries involve multiple columns in the WHERE clause or JOIN operations.

Creating and Managing Indexes

To create an index, you typically use SQL statements like `CREATE INDEX`. The exact syntax varies between database systems, so consult your DBMS documentation for specific instructions. Here's a simplified example of creating a B-Tree index on the `email` column of a `users` table in SQL Server:

```sql
-- Creating a B-Tree index on the 'email' column
CREATE INDEX IX_Users_Email ON users (email);
```

While indexing can significantly boost query performance, it's essential to be mindful of potential downsides:

1. Storage Overhead: Indexes consume disk space. In cases of excessive indexing, this overhead can become substantial.

2. Maintenance Overhead: Indexes need to be maintained whenever data is modified. INSERT, UPDATE, and DELETE operations on indexed tables can become slower due to index maintenance.

3. Query Plan Changes: The DBMS optimizer uses indexes to determine the most efficient query plan. However, the presence of indexes can sometimes lead the optimizer to choose suboptimal plans. Regularly review query execution plans to identify any performance regressions.

4. Index Fragmentation: Over time, indexes can become fragmented, impacting query performance. Periodically rebuild or reorganize indexes to address fragmentation.

Monitoring Index Performance

To ensure that your indexes are serving their purpose and not causing performance issues, it's crucial to monitor their performance regularly. Here are some steps to consider:

1. Index Usage Analysis: Monitor which indexes are being used by your queries. Unused indexes may be candidates for removal.

2. Query Performance Metrics: Track query execution times and resource usage to identify queries that may benefit from additional indexing.

3. Fragmentation Analysis: Regularly check for index fragmentation and take action as needed.

4. Database Growth: As your database grows, revisit your indexing strategy to ensure it remains effective.

Conclusion

Effectively utilizing indexes is a core strategy for optimizing SQL statement performance. When chosen and configured correctly, indexes can significantly enhance query execution speed. However, it's essential to strike a balance between indexing for performance and managing the associated overhead. Regular monitoring and maintenance are key to ensuring that indexes continue to support optimal database performance.

2.4.2. Optimizing Joins and Subqueries

Joins and subqueries are fundamental components of SQL queries, enabling us to retrieve data from multiple tables and apply logical conditions. However, poorly optimized joins and subqueries can severely impact query performance. In this section, we will explore strategies for optimizing these essential SQL elements to enhance overall query execution speed.

Understanding Joins

A join is a SQL operation that combines rows from two or more tables based on a related column between them. There are several types of joins, including INNER JOIN, LEFT JOIN (or LEFT OUTER JOIN), RIGHT JOIN (or RIGHT OUTER JOIN), and FULL JOIN (or FULL OUTER JOIN). Each join type serves a specific purpose:

- **INNER JOIN:** Returns only the rows with matching values in both tables. It filters out non-matching rows.

- **LEFT JOIN:** Returns all rows from the left table (the first table listed) and the matching rows from the right table (the second table listed). If there is no match in the right table, NULL values are returned.

- **RIGHT JOIN:** Similar to LEFT JOIN but returns all rows from the right table and matching rows from the left table.

- **FULL JOIN:** Returns all rows when there is a match in either the left or right table. When there is no match, NULL values are returned for the non-matching side.

Optimizing Joins

1. Use Proper Indexing: Ensure that columns involved in join conditions are appropriately indexed. Indexes on foreign keys and columns used in WHERE clauses can significantly improve join performance.

2. Limit the Result Set: Retrieve only the columns you need. Unnecessary columns in the result set can increase data transfer and processing overhead.

3. Choose the Right Join Type: Select the appropriate join type for your query. If you only need matching rows, use INNER JOIN. If you want to include non-matching rows, consider LEFT JOIN or RIGHT JOIN.

4. Avoid Excessive Joins: Minimize the number of joins in your query. Complex join operations can quickly degrade performance. Consider breaking down queries into multiple steps or using temporary tables if necessary.

5. Use EXISTS and IN: In some cases, using EXISTS or IN subqueries can be more efficient than joins. Experiment with these alternatives when optimizing queries.

6. Analyze Query Execution Plans: Most database systems provide tools to analyze query execution plans. Review these plans to identify potential bottlenecks or inefficient joins.

Understanding Subqueries

A subquery, also known as a nested query or inner query, is a query embedded within another SQL statement. Subqueries can appear in various parts of a query, such as the SELECT clause, FROM clause, or WHERE clause. They are used to retrieve data that will be used in the main query's criteria or calculations.

Optimizing Subqueries

1. Use Correlated Subqueries Sparingly: Correlated subqueries are subqueries that depend on the outer query for their results. They can be slow, especially when dealing with large datasets. Try to rewrite correlated subqueries as joins when possible.

2. Ensure Subquery Returns Minimal Data: Subqueries should return only the necessary data. Avoid retrieving excessive columns or rows if they are not essential for the main query.

3. Use EXISTS and IN: EXISTS and IN subqueries can often be optimized by the database engine more efficiently than standard subqueries.

4. Evaluate the Query Execution Plan: As with joins, analyze the execution plan generated by the database for subqueries. It can provide insights into potential performance improvements.

Example: Optimizing a Subquery

Suppose we have two tables, `orders` and `order_items`, and we want to find all orders where the total order amount exceeds $1,000. Initially, we might write a subquery like this:

```sql
SELECT order_id
FROM orders
WHERE order_id IN (
    SELECT order_id
    FROM order_items
    GROUP BY order_id
```

```
        HAVING SUM(item_price) > 1000
);
```

This subquery finds orders with a total amount over $1,000 by summing the item prices in the `order_items` table. However, it's a correlated subquery since it depends on the outer query's `order_id`. We can optimize this query by using a join instead of a subquery:

```sql
SELECT o.order_id
FROM orders o
JOIN (
    SELECT order_id
    FROM order_items
    GROUP BY order_id
    HAVING SUM(item_price) > 1000
) oi ON o.order_id = oi.order_id;
```

By using a join, we eliminate the correlated subquery and potentially improve query performance.

Conclusion

Optimizing joins and subqueries is essential for enhancing SQL statement performance. Proper indexing, selecting the right join types, and minimizing the use of correlated subqueries are crucial strategies for achieving efficient SQL queries. Regularly analyze query execution plans and consider alternative approaches to improve your SQL query performance.

2.4.3. Reducing Overhead with Query Simplification

Query simplification is a critical aspect of SQL performance tuning. It involves streamlining SQL statements to eliminate unnecessary complexity and reduce overhead. Simplified queries not only execute faster but are also easier to maintain. In this section, we will explore the principles of query simplification and provide practical examples of how to achieve it.

Why Query Simplification Matters

Complex SQL queries can be challenging to debug, optimize, and maintain. They often involve numerous joins, subqueries, and unnecessary calculations, leading to increased processing time and resource utilization. By simplifying queries, you can:

1. Improve Readability: Simplified queries are easier for developers to understand, reducing the likelihood of errors and making it simpler to collaborate on projects.

2. Enhance Performance: Reducing unnecessary calculations and data retrieval leads to faster query execution times and less strain on the database server.

3. Facilitate Maintenance: Simplified queries are easier to maintain and troubleshoot, saving time and effort in the long run.

Now, let's delve into various techniques to simplify SQL queries.

1. Select Only Necessary Columns

When retrieving data from a table, specify only the columns you need. Avoid using `SELECT *` to fetch all columns when you require only a subset of them. This reduces data transfer overhead and improves query performance.

Example:

Consider a table named `employees` with columns `employee_id`, `first_name`, `last_name`, `email`, `hire_date`, and `salary`. If you need to retrieve the names and email addresses of employees hired after a certain date, use the following simplified query:

```sql
SELECT first_name, last_name, email
FROM employees
WHERE hire_date > '2023-01-01';
```

2. Minimize the Use of Functions

Excessive use of functions in SQL queries can introduce unnecessary complexity. While functions are essential for some calculations, they should be used judiciously. Try to perform computations in the application layer when possible, as it can be more efficient.

Example:

Suppose you want to retrieve the total number of employees. Instead of using the `COUNT()` function, you can simplify the query as follows:

```sql
SELECT COUNT(*) AS total_employees
FROM employees;
```

3. Avoid Excessive Joins

While joins are essential for combining data from multiple tables, too many joins in a single query can lead to performance issues. Evaluate whether all joined tables are necessary for the query's purpose.

Example:

Consider a scenario where you need to retrieve customer orders along with their associated product details and shipping information. Instead of joining all these tables in a single query, consider breaking it down into multiple queries or using temporary tables for intermediate results.

4. Reduce Subqueries

Subqueries can add complexity to SQL statements. Whenever possible, aim to simplify subqueries by using joins or other alternatives.

Example:

Suppose you want to find employees with salaries greater than the average salary in their department. Instead of using a subquery, you can achieve this with a join:

```sql
SELECT e.employee_id, e.first_name, e.last_name, e.salary
FROM employees e
JOIN (
    SELECT department_id, AVG(salary) AS avg_salary
    FROM employees
    GROUP BY department_id
) d ON e.department_id = d.department_id
WHERE e.salary > d.avg_salary;
```

5. Use Common Table Expressions (CTEs)

CTEs allow you to define temporary result sets within your query, making it more readable and maintainable. They can also help simplify complex queries.

Example:

Suppose you need to find the total revenue generated by each product category. Using a CTE can make your query more straightforward:

```sql
WITH CategoryRevenue AS (
```

```
SELECT p.category_id, SUM(o.quantity * o.unit_price) AS total_revenue

FROM orders o

JOIN products p ON o.product_id = p.product_id

GROUP BY p.category_id
)
SELECT c.category_name, cr.total_revenue

FROM categories c

JOIN CategoryRevenue cr ON c.category_id = cr.category_id;
```

6. Avoid Unnecessary Sorting and Ordering

Sorting results can be computationally expensive. If you don't need sorted data, remove `ORDER BY` clauses from your query to improve performance.

Example:

If you only need to retrieve the most recently hired employees and don't require them to be sorted, remove the unnecessary `ORDER BY`:

```sql
SELECT first_name, last_name, hire_date

FROM employees

WHERE hire_date > '2023-01-01';
```

Conclusion

Query simplification is a fundamental technique in SQL performance tuning. By adhering to the principles outlined here, you can create more efficient and maintainable SQL statements. Remember that readability, performance, and maintainability are all essential aspects of query optimization, and simplification plays a pivotal role in achieving these goals.

In the next section, we will explore another critical aspect of SQL performance tuning: index optimization. We'll learn how to use indexes effectively to enhance query performance.

PART III
Utilizing SQL Performance Tuning Tools

3.1 SQL Investigation and Analysis Tools

3.1.1. Introduction to SQL Profilers

SQL profilers are indispensable tools in the arsenal of SQL performance tuners. They allow you to capture and analyze the SQL statements and events occurring within your database system. Profilers provide detailed insights into query execution, resource consumption, and potential bottlenecks, making them essential for diagnosing and optimizing SQL performance issues.

In this section, we'll introduce you to SQL profilers, explaining what they are, why they are essential, and how to effectively utilize them in your SQL performance tuning efforts.

What Is a SQL Profiler?

A SQL profiler, often referred to as a database profiler or query profiler, is a software tool designed to monitor and record SQL statements and related events as they execute on a database server. It captures a wealth of information about each query, such as the query text, execution time, query plans, and resource usage.

SQL profilers serve several critical functions:

1. Query Monitoring: Profilers track the execution of SQL queries in real-time, allowing you to see which queries are running, how often, and their resource consumption.

2. Performance Analysis: Profilers provide detailed insights into query performance, helping you identify slow-running queries, inefficient execution plans, and potential bottlenecks.

3. Troubleshooting: When unexpected behavior or errors occur in your database, profilers can help pinpoint the root cause by capturing the exact queries and events leading up to the issue.

4. Optimization: By analyzing the data collected by profilers, you can make informed decisions about query optimization, index creation, and database schema improvements.

Why Use SQL Profilers?

SQL profilers offer numerous benefits for database administrators, developers, and performance tuners. Here are some compelling reasons to use them:

1. Performance Optimization: Profilers help you identify poorly performing queries and bottlenecks, enabling you to take corrective actions and enhance overall system performance.

2. Real-time Monitoring: You can monitor SQL statements as they execute in real-time, making it easier to detect and address issues promptly.

3. Resource Usage Analysis: Profilers provide insights into resource consumption, including CPU, memory, and I/O usage, helping you optimize resource utilization.

4. Query Debugging: When troubleshooting database issues or unexpected results, profilers offer a detailed history of query executions, allowing you to trace problematic queries.

5. Query Tuning: Profilers enable you to evaluate the impact of query modifications, indexes, and database schema changes on performance.

Using SQL Profilers

Now, let's explore how to use SQL profilers effectively. While the specific steps may vary depending on the database management system (DBMS) you are using, the general process remains consistent.

1. Selecting a Profiler Tool: Choose a SQL profiler tool compatible with your DBMS. Common options include SQL Server Profiler (for Microsoft SQL Server), Oracle SQL Developer (for Oracle Database), and pgBadger (for PostgreSQL).

2. Connect to the Database: Launch the profiler tool and establish a connection to the database you want to monitor.

3. Configure Profiling Options: Configure the profiler to capture the specific events and information you need. Common configuration options include:

  - **Events to Capture:** Select the types of events to monitor, such as query execution, login/logout, and errors.

  - **Filters:** Define filters to capture data for specific databases, users, or applications.

  - **Output Format:** Specify how you want the profiler to display or save captured data.

4. Start Profiling: Begin profiling by starting the capture process. The profiler will record relevant events and queries as they occur on the database server.

5. Analyze Profiling Data: Once you've captured sufficient data, stop the profiler and analyze the results. Look for:

  - Slow-running queries with high execution times.

  - Queries causing excessive resource utilization (CPU, memory, I/O).

- Frequent query patterns that may benefit from optimization.

6. Optimization Actions: Based on your analysis, take appropriate actions to optimize the identified queries. This may involve rewriting queries, creating or modifying indexes, or adjusting database configurations.

Example: Using SQL Server Profiler

Let's walk through a simplified example of using SQL Server Profiler, a commonly used tool for Microsoft SQL Server:

1. Launch SQL Server Profiler: Start SQL Server Profiler from your SQL Server Management Studio (SSMS) or as a standalone application.

2. Connect to SQL Server: Connect to the SQL Server instance you want to profile. You'll need the necessary permissions to capture trace data.

3. Create a New Trace: In SQL Server Profiler, create a new trace by clicking "File" > "New Trace." Configure the trace properties, including the events to capture, filters, and output options.

4. Start the Trace: Start the trace, and it will begin capturing events as they occur on the SQL Server.

5. Analyze Captured Data: Allow the trace to run for a period during which it captures relevant data. Stop the trace when you've collected sufficient information.

6. Review Query Execution: In the captured data, you can review the execution times, query text, and related information for each query.

7. Identify Performance Issues: Look for queries with long execution times, high CPU or memory usage, or frequent occurrences.

8. Optimize Queries: Based on your findings, work on optimizing the identified queries. You may rewrite queries for better performance, add or modify indexes, or fine-tune database settings.

9. Monitor Progress: After implementing optimizations, continue to monitor query performance to ensure improvements have been achieved.

SQL profilers are invaluable tools for database professionals, aiding in the identification and resolution of performance bottlenecks. When used effectively, they contribute to the overall health and efficiency of database systems.

In the next section, we will delve deeper into popular SQL performance tuning tools beyond profilers, expanding your toolkit for optimizing SQL performance.

3.1.2. Query Execution Tracing

Query execution tracing is a vital technique in SQL performance tuning, providing detailed insights into how SQL queries are processed by the database engine. It allows you to trace the execution path of queries, monitor their performance, and identify areas for optimization. In this section, we'll explore query execution tracing in-depth, covering its importance, methodologies, and tools for various database systems.

Why Query Execution Tracing Matters

Query execution tracing is essential for the following reasons:

1. Performance Profiling: Tracing allows you to profile the execution of SQL queries in real-time or retrospectively. You can pinpoint bottlenecks, slow-performing queries, and resource-intensive operations.

2. Problem Diagnosis: When queries produce unexpected results or errors, tracing helps identify the exact sequence of events leading to the issue, making debugging more efficient.

3. Optimization Insights: Tracing provides a wealth of information about query execution plans, index usage, and resource consumption. This data is crucial for fine-tuning queries and database structures.

4. Benchmarking: You can compare the performance of different query versions, indexes, or configurations by tracing their executions and analyzing the collected metrics.

Query Execution Tracing Methodologies

There are two primary methodologies for query execution tracing:

1. Real-time Tracing: This method captures query execution data as queries are run in real-time. It's useful for monitoring and diagnosing ongoing performance issues.

2. Retrospective Tracing: Retrospective tracing records query executions over a specific period or for a set of predefined queries. It's ideal for in-depth performance analysis and optimization.

Tools for Query Execution Tracing

Query execution tracing tools vary depending on your database management system (DBMS). Let's explore how to perform query execution tracing for popular DBMSs: Microsoft SQL Server, Oracle Database, and PostgreSQL.

Microsoft SQL Server: SQL Server Profiler

SQL Server Profiler is a built-in tool for tracing query execution in SQL Server. Here's how to use it:

1. Launch SQL Server Profiler: Open SQL Server Profiler from SQL Server Management Studio (SSMS) or as a standalone application.

2. Create a New Trace: Click "File" > "New Trace" to create a new trace. Configure the trace properties, including events, columns, and filters.

3. Start the Trace: Start the trace to begin capturing query execution data. You can monitor queries in real-time or save trace data for later analysis.

4. Analyze Traced Data: Review the captured data to identify slow-running queries, resource-intensive operations, and execution plans.

5. Optimization: Based on your analysis, optimize queries, add indexes, or adjust configurations to enhance performance.

Oracle Database: Oracle Trace

Oracle provides tracing capabilities through Oracle Trace. Here's how to trace queries in Oracle:

1. Enable Oracle Trace: Use the `ALTER SESSION` command to enable tracing for your session:

```sql
ALTER SESSION SET SQL_TRACE = TRUE;
```

2. Run Queries: Execute the queries you want to trace in the same session with tracing enabled.

3. Generate Trace Files: Oracle generates trace files containing query execution data. These files are typically located in the Oracle diagnostic directory.

4. Analyze Trace Files: Use the Oracle Trace File Analyzer (TFA) or manually review the trace files to examine query performance and execution details.

5. Optimization: Apply query optimization techniques based on the insights gained from trace files.

PostgreSQL: pg_stat_statements and pg_stat_activity

PostgreSQL offers query execution tracing through built-in views. Here's how to trace queries in PostgreSQL:

1. Enable pg_stat_statements: Ensure the `pg_stat_statements` extension is enabled in your PostgreSQL database:

```sql
CREATE EXTENSION pg_stat_statements;
```

2. Enable Track Activities: Track activities by setting `track_activities = on` in your PostgreSQL configuration file.

3. Run Queries: Execute the queries you want to trace in your PostgreSQL database.

4. Query Analysis: Use the `pg_stat_statements` view to query statistics about executed queries. You can also monitor ongoing query activity using `pg_stat_activity`.

5. Optimization: Based on the collected statistics, optimize queries, consider indexing, or fine-tune database settings.

Query Execution Tracing Best Practices

To make the most of query execution tracing, follow these best practices:

1. Use Sampling: In high-traffic environments, sampling queries can reduce overhead. Instead of tracing every query, capture a representative sample.

2. Set Clear Goals: Define specific goals for tracing, such as identifying slow queries or monitoring resource usage.

3. Focus on Critical Queries: Prioritize tracing for queries that have the most significant impact on performance or are part of critical business processes.

4. Regular Monitoring: Establish a routine for tracing and monitoring query performance to catch issues early.

5. Document Findings: Document your tracing findings and the optimizations applied for future reference.

Example: Query Execution Tracing with SQL Server Profiler

Suppose you have a SQL Server database and want to trace the execution of a slow-running query. Follow these steps using SQL Server Profiler:

1. Launch SQL Server Profiler: Open SQL Server Management Studio (SSMS) and go to "Tools" > "SQL Server Profiler."

2. Create a New Trace: Click "File" > "New Trace." In the "Events Selection" tab, choose "TSQL" under "Stored Procedures" and "SQL:BatchCompleted" under "SQL Statements." This captures query executions.

3. Start the Trace: Click the green "Run" button to start the trace.

4. Run the Query: In SSMS, execute the query you want to trace.

5. Analyze the Trace: SQL Server Profiler will display the traced query execution events in real-time. You can review execution times, read and write operations, and query text.

6. Optimize: Based on the trace data, optimize the query as needed. This may involve rewriting the query, adding indexes, or adjusting database settings.

By following these steps, you can effectively use SQL Server Profiler to trace query executions and improve the performance of your SQL Server database.

Conclusion

Query execution tracing is a powerful technique for identifying and optimizing SQL queries that impact the performance of your database systems. Whether you're using Microsoft SQL Server, Oracle Database, PostgreSQL, or another DBMS, understanding how to trace queries and interpret the collected data is essential for maintaining efficient and responsive database environments. By following best practices and using the appropriate tracing tools, you can uncover performance bottlenecks, diagnose issues, and implement optimizations that enhance the overall performance of your database systems.

3.1.3. Performance Dashboard and Reports

SQL performance tuning often involves working with a variety of tools and utilities that provide insights into database performance. One such tool is the Performance Dashboard, which is available in Microsoft SQL Server. In this section, we will explore the Performance Dashboard, its significance in SQL performance tuning, and how to effectively use it to analyze performance metrics and generate reports.

Why Use the Performance Dashboard?

The Performance Dashboard is a valuable feature in SQL Server that offers a consolidated view of database performance metrics and helps database administrators and developers identify performance bottlenecks and areas that require optimization. Here's why it matters:

1. Comprehensive Performance Data: The Performance Dashboard aggregates data from various sources within SQL Server, providing a comprehensive overview of database performance.

2. Real-time Monitoring: You can monitor performance metrics in real-time, making it easier to identify and address performance issues as they occur.

3. Historical Analysis: The Performance Dashboard also maintains historical data, enabling you to analyze performance trends over time.

4. User-Friendly Interface: It presents performance data through a user-friendly and visually appealing interface, making it accessible to a wide range of users.

Accessing the Performance Dashboard

To access the Performance Dashboard in SQL Server, follow these steps:

1. Connect to SQL Server: Launch SQL Server Management Studio (SSMS) and connect to your SQL Server instance.

2. Enable the Performance Dashboard: Before you can use the Performance Dashboard, you need to enable it. Run the following query:

```sql
-- Enable the Performance Dashboard
USE master;
GO
```

```
EXEC sp_configure 'show advanced options', 1;

RECONFIGURE;

EXEC sp_configure 'external scripts enabled', 1;

RECONFIGURE;

EXEC sp_configure 'show advanced options', 0;

RECONFIGURE;

```
```

3. Access the Dashboard: In SSMS, navigate to the "View" menu, point to "Dashboard," and select "Performance Dashboard." This opens the Performance Dashboard window.

Understanding the Performance Dashboard

The Performance Dashboard is organized into several sections, each providing specific insights into database performance. Here are the key sections you'll find:

1. Overall Summary: The top section provides a summary of CPU utilization, I/O utilization, and other key performance indicators.

2. Database I/O: This section displays information about database I/O operations, including read and write latencies.

3. Recent Expensive Queries: You can view a list of recent queries that consumed the most resources, such as CPU or I/O.

4. Wait Statistics: Wait statistics help you identify the most common reasons for query waits and performance bottlenecks.
```

5. File I/O: Information about file I/O operations, including file latency and read/write operations, is presented here.

6. Performance Reports: The Performance Dashboard also provides links to various performance reports that offer more detailed information about different aspects of performance.

Analyzing Performance Data

To effectively analyze performance data using the Performance Dashboard, follow these steps:

1. Monitor in Real-Time: Keep the Performance Dashboard open to monitor performance metrics in real-time. Pay attention to any sudden spikes or anomalies.

2. Investigate Expensive Queries: Review the "Recent Expensive Queries" section to identify queries that are causing performance issues. You can click on a query to see its execution plan and details.

3. Examine Wait Statistics: Check the "Wait Statistics" section to determine if there are frequent wait events. Address the most common wait events to improve overall performance.

4. Use Performance Reports: Explore the performance reports linked in the dashboard for more in-depth analysis of specific areas like query performance, index usage, and more.

Generating Reports

The Performance Dashboard allows you to generate reports based on the collected performance data. Reports offer a more detailed view of performance metrics and can be shared with colleagues or stakeholders. Here's how to generate reports:

1. Click on the "Performance Reports" section of the dashboard.

2. Choose the type of report you want to generate, such as "Performance Overview" or "Resource Waits."

3. Customize report parameters, if necessary.

4. Click "View Report" to generate and view the report.

5. You can export the report to various formats, including PDF, Excel, or Word.

Optimizing with the Performance Dashboard

Once you've identified performance issues using the Performance Dashboard, take action to optimize your SQL Server database:

1. Optimize Queries: Address poorly performing queries by rewriting them, adding indexes, or adjusting query execution plans.

2. Monitor Regularly: Continuously monitor your database's performance using the Performance Dashboard to catch and resolve issues promptly.

3. Use Indexing Wisely: Analyze index usage and consider adding, modifying, or removing indexes to improve query performance.

4. Tune Hardware: Evaluate server hardware to ensure it meets the demands of your database workload. Consider upgrading hardware if necessary.

5. Review Configuration: Review and adjust SQL Server configuration settings to optimize performance.

Conclusion

The Performance Dashboard is a powerful tool within SQL Server that simplifies the process of monitoring, analyzing, and optimizing database performance. By regularly using this tool to assess your database's health and performance, you can proactively identify and resolve issues, ensuring that your SQL Server databases operate efficiently and provide optimal performance for your applications.

3.2 Popular SQL Performance Tuning Tools

3.2.1. SQL Server Query Store

SQL Server Query Store is a powerful tool that assists database administrators and developers in monitoring query performance, identifying bottlenecks, and optimizing SQL queries. In this section, we will explore the significance of SQL Server Query Store, how to enable it, and how to use it effectively to improve database performance.

Why Use SQL Server Query Store?

SQL Server Query Store is essential for performance tuning for several reasons:

1. Historical Query Data: Query Store maintains historical data about executed queries, allowing you to analyze query performance over time. This historical perspective is crucial for identifying trends and recurring issues.

2. Query Execution Plans: It stores execution plans for queries, making it easier to understand how SQL Server executes queries and providing insight into plan changes over time.

3. Performance Metrics: Query Store captures various performance metrics for queries, such as CPU usage, execution time, and I/O statistics, helping you pinpoint performance bottlenecks.

4. Query Regressions: You can easily identify query regressions, where query performance deteriorates over time, enabling you to take corrective action.

Enabling SQL Server Query Store

Before you can use SQL Server Query Store, you need to enable it for your database. Here's how to do it:

1. Connect to SQL Server: Launch SQL Server Management Studio (SSMS) and connect to your SQL Server instance.

2. Select Database: In Object Explorer, right-click on your target database and select "Properties."

3. Enable Query Store: In the "Database Properties" dialog, navigate to the "Query Store" page. Set the "Operation Mode" to "Read Write" to enable Query Store for your database.

4. Configure Data Retention: Specify how long you want to retain query and runtime statistics data. You can choose between a set number of days or unlimited retention.

5. Click OK: Save your changes, and Query Store will be enabled for the selected database.

Using SQL Server Query Store

Once Query Store is enabled, you can start using it to monitor and optimize query performance:

1. Monitoring Query Performance:

   - Open SSMS and connect to your SQL Server instance.

   - In Object Explorer, expand your database, navigate to the "Query Store" node, and select "Top Resource Consuming Queries."

   - You can view a list of queries sorted by resource consumption, including CPU usage, execution time, and more. This helps you identify poorly performing queries.

2. Query Plan Analysis:

- In Query Store, select "Top Resource Consuming Queries."

- Click on a query to view its execution plan history. This allows you to see how query execution plans change over time, which is crucial for query optimization.

3. Identifying Regressed Queries:

- Use the "Regressed Queries" report in Query Store to identify queries that have become slower over time.

- Analyze the regressed queries to understand why they are performing poorly and take corrective actions.

4. Force Query Plan: If you identify a query with a suboptimal execution plan, you can use Query Store to force a specific execution plan for that query, ensuring it performs optimally.

5. Automatic Tuning: In some cases, SQL Server can automatically identify and fix query performance issues using Query Store. This feature, known as Automatic Tuning, can be enabled for specific databases.

6. Retaining and Purging Data: Query Store retains historical data about query performance. Periodically, you may want to purge older data to manage storage. You can do this in the Query Store settings.

Best Practices for Using Query Store:

To effectively use SQL Server Query Store, consider these best practices:

1. Regular Monitoring: Make query performance monitoring part of your routine database maintenance to catch issues early.

2. Review Execution Plans: Analyze query execution plans to understand how queries are processed and to identify areas for optimization.

3. Use Plan Forcing Sparingly: While forcing query plans can be helpful, use this feature judiciously, as it may have unintended consequences.

4. Data Retention: Configure data retention settings based on your organization's needs and available storage.

5. Work with Query Statistics: Dive into query statistics to pinpoint performance bottlenecks and areas for optimization.

6. Leverage Automatic Tuning: If appropriate, consider enabling Automatic Tuning for databases to automate query performance improvements.

SQL Server Query Store is a valuable tool for database administrators and developers, providing insights into query performance and historical data that can lead to significant performance improvements. By following best practices and regularly monitoring your database using Query Store, you can ensure your SQL Server databases operate efficiently and deliver optimal performance.

3.2.2. Oracle SQL Tuning Advisor

Oracle SQL Tuning Advisor is a robust tool that helps database administrators and developers optimize SQL queries and improve the overall performance of Oracle databases. In this section, we will delve into the significance of Oracle SQL Tuning Advisor, how to use it effectively, and best practices for query optimization.

Why Use Oracle SQL Tuning Advisor?

Oracle SQL Tuning Advisor offers several advantages for database performance tuning:

1. Automatic Query Tuning: It can automatically identify poorly performing SQL statements and suggest improvements, making it suitable for both novice and experienced database professionals.

2. Comprehensive Recommendations: The advisor provides detailed recommendations for query optimization, including creating indexes, restructuring SQL statements, and using hints to guide the query optimizer.

3. Integration with Oracle Database: SQL Tuning Advisor is integrated with Oracle Database, simplifying the optimization process and ensuring compatibility.

4. Performance Monitoring: It continually monitors SQL statements, making it possible to address performance issues as they arise.

Using Oracle SQL Tuning Advisor

To utilize Oracle SQL Tuning Advisor effectively, follow these steps:

1. Access SQL Tuning Advisor:

  - Connect to your Oracle Database using SQL*Plus or another Oracle client.

2. Identify the SQL Statements:

  - Determine which SQL statements you want to optimize. These may be queries that are critical for your application or statements that have exhibited poor performance.

3. Create a SQL Tuning Task:

- Use the `DBMS_SQLTUNE.CREATE_TUNING_TASK` procedure to create a tuning task. This task specifies the SQL statements to tune and other parameters.

4. Execute the Task:

- Begin the SQL tuning task using the `DBMS_SQLTUNE.EXECUTE_TUNING_TASK` procedure. This initiates the analysis of the specified SQL statements.

5. Review Recommendations:

- After the task completes, you can retrieve the tuning recommendations using the `DBMS_SQLTUNE.REPORT_TUNING_TASK` procedure or by querying the `DBA_ADVISOR_TASKS` and `DBA_ADVISOR_FINDINGS` views.

6. Implement Recommendations:

- Act on the recommendations provided by the SQL Tuning Advisor. These may include creating indexes, adjusting SQL code, or using hints.

7. Monitor Performance:

- Continuously monitor the performance of the tuned SQL statements to ensure that the recommendations have improved query execution.

Best Practices for Using Oracle SQL Tuning Advisor:

To maximize the benefits of Oracle SQL Tuning Advisor, consider these best practices:

1. Select Relevant SQL Statements: Focus on SQL statements that have a significant impact on your application's performance. Tuning less critical queries may not yield substantial benefits.

2. Regularly Schedule Tuning Tasks: Set up a schedule to run SQL tuning tasks regularly, especially in dynamic database environments where query performance may change over time.

3. Evaluate Recommendations: Review tuning recommendations carefully. Not all recommendations may be suitable for implementation, so use your judgment to prioritize and apply them.

4. Test in a Controlled Environment: Before implementing recommendations in a production environment, test them in a controlled setting to ensure they don't introduce regressions or other issues.

5. Track Performance Changes: After applying recommendations, monitor query performance to confirm improvements and make further adjustments if necessary.

6. Use Bind Variables: Encourage developers to use bind variables in their SQL code, as it helps Oracle to reuse execution plans and optimize queries more effectively.

7. Regular Database Maintenance: Perform regular database maintenance tasks such as indexing, statistics collection, and partitioning, as these can have a significant impact on query performance.

8. Stay Informed: Keep up-to-date with Oracle Database releases and SQL Tuning Advisor enhancements to take advantage of new features and improvements.

Oracle SQL Tuning Advisor is a valuable tool for optimizing SQL queries in Oracle databases. By following best practices and incorporating it into your database maintenance routine, you can ensure that your Oracle database performs optimally, delivering fast and efficient query execution.

3.2.3. MySQL Performance Schema

MySQL Performance Schema is a powerful tool for monitoring and optimizing the performance of MySQL database servers. It provides detailed insights into the internal workings of MySQL, helping database administrators and developers identify performance bottlenecks, tune queries, and improve overall system performance. In this section, we'll explore the significance of MySQL Performance Schema, how to use it effectively, and best practices for MySQL performance tuning.

Why Use MySQL Performance Schema?

MySQL Performance Schema offers several benefits for database performance tuning:

1. Granular Performance Data: It collects detailed information about query execution, resource consumption, and wait events, allowing for precise performance analysis.

2. Real-time Monitoring: Performance Schema provides real-time statistics, making it possible to identify performance issues as they occur.

3. Query Profiling: You can profile individual SQL statements to understand their resource consumption and execution patterns.

4. Resource Tracking: It tracks resource utilization, helping you identify bottlenecks related to CPU, memory, disk I/O, and more.

5. Wait Event Analysis: Performance Schema reports on wait events, which are crucial for diagnosing performance problems related to contention and resource contention.

Using MySQL Performance Schema

To leverage MySQL Performance Schema effectively, follow these steps:

1. Enable Performance Schema:

 - Performance Schema is disabled by default in MySQL. To enable it, add `performance-schema=ON` to your MySQL configuration file (`my.cnf` or `my.ini`) and restart the MySQL server.

2. Select the Desired Instrumentation: Performance Schema allows you to select which events and instruments to monitor. Configure your MySQL instance to collect the information that's relevant to your performance tuning goals.

3. Query Performance Schema Tables: MySQL Performance Schema stores performance data in various tables. You can query these tables to retrieve performance information.

4. Analyze Query Execution: Use the `events_statements_*` tables to analyze the performance of SQL statements. You can identify slow queries, examine execution plans, and find resource-intensive queries.

5. Resource Monitoring: Check the `events_waits_*` tables to monitor resource usage and wait events. This helps you identify bottlenecks related to resources like CPU, I/O, and locks.

6. Profile Specific SQL Statements: Utilize the `events_statements_current` and `events_statements_history` tables to profile individual SQL statements. This allows you to see detailed statistics for each query.

7. Use the Sys Schema: MySQL provides the sys schema, a set of views and stored procedures that simplify the querying of Performance Schema data. It's a user-friendly way to access performance information.

Best Practices for Using MySQL Performance Schema:

To make the most of MySQL Performance Schema, consider these best practices:

1. Start with Relevant Events: Enable only the performance schema events that are relevant to your specific tuning objectives to minimize overhead.

2. Regularly Review Performance Data: Schedule regular reviews of Performance Schema data to detect emerging performance issues and take proactive measures.

3. Set Up Performance Alerts: Implement alerting mechanisms based on Performance Schema data to notify you of critical performance problems in real-time.

4. Profile Under Load: Profile queries and resources under production-like loads to ensure accurate performance analysis.

5. Use Performance Schema Reports: MySQL provides several performance schema reports that summarize important performance metrics. Explore and use these reports to gain insights quickly.

6. Consider Sys Schema: Take advantage of the sys schema's views and stored procedures for easier querying and reporting on Performance Schema data.

7. Document and Share Findings: Document your performance tuning efforts and share them with your team to ensure that everyone benefits from the insights gained.

MySQL Performance Schema is an invaluable tool for optimizing MySQL database performance. By using it effectively and following best practices, you can identify and address performance bottlenecks, resulting in faster and more efficient MySQL database operations.

3.3 Implementing SQL Performance Testing

3.3.1. Creating Realistic Test Environments

Effective SQL performance testing is a crucial step in the process of optimizing your database-driven applications. By creating realistic test environments, you can simulate real-world scenarios, identify performance bottlenecks, and fine-tune your SQL queries for optimal performance. In this section, we will explore the importance of realistic test environments, how to set them up, and best practices for conducting SQL performance testing.

Why Realistic Test Environments Matter:

Realistic test environments are essential for several reasons:

1. Accurate Results: Simulating actual usage conditions ensures that your performance testing results closely mirror what your application will experience in production.

2. Bottleneck Discovery: A realistic environment helps you identify bottlenecks and performance issues that may not be apparent in isolated or idealized test scenarios.

3. User Experience: Testing in a true-to-life environment allows you to gauge the user experience accurately, helping you meet user expectations.

4. Proactive Optimization: Early detection of performance problems in a test environment enables proactive optimization, reducing the chances of performance issues occurring in production.

Creating a Realistic Test Environment:

To create a realistic test environment for SQL performance testing, follow these steps:

1. Understand Production Environment: Gain a deep understanding of your production environment, including hardware specifications, database configurations, and workload patterns.

2. Database Backup and Restore: Create a backup of your production database and restore it to your test environment. This ensures that your test database contains realistic data.

3. Test Data Generation: Generate realistic test data that resembles your production data. Consider using data generation tools or scripts to populate your database with representative data.

4. Application Simulation: Simulate user interactions and application workflows that mimic real-world usage. Use load testing tools to simulate concurrent user activity.

5. Network and Infrastructure: Ensure that the network conditions and infrastructure in your test environment match those of your production environment as closely as possible.

6. Configuration Matching: Configure your database, web server, and application settings to match the production environment's configurations.

Best Practices for SQL Performance Testing in Realistic Environments:

1. Use Test Data Subsets: In large databases, testing with a subset of data can be more practical. Ensure that your subset is representative of production data.

2. Gradual Load Testing: Start with a small load and gradually increase it to simulate user growth. Monitor performance at each load level to identify breaking points.

3. Realistic Workloads: Design test scenarios that mimic real user workflows, including a mix of read and write operations, complex queries, and typical transaction patterns.

4. Monitoring and Profiling: Implement performance monitoring and profiling tools to collect data during tests. Monitor resource utilization, query execution times, and system metrics.

5. Scripted Testing: Automate your testing process with scripts that simulate user behavior and workloads. This ensures repeatability and consistency.

6. Identify Bottlenecks: Use SQL profiling and monitoring tools to identify performance bottlenecks, such as slow queries, locking issues, or resource constraints.

7. Response Time Analysis: Pay close attention to response times during testing. Set acceptable response time thresholds and flag any queries or operations that exceed them.

8. Baseline Metrics: Establish baseline performance metrics in your test environment. This will serve as a reference point for future tests and allow you to measure improvements.

9. Load Balancing: Test load balancing and failover mechanisms if your production environment uses them. Ensure they function as expected under load.

10. Documentation: Document your testing procedures, results, and any issues encountered. This documentation is invaluable for future reference and troubleshooting.

Creating a realistic test environment and conducting SQL performance testing is a proactive approach to ensuring your database-driven applications perform well in production. By following best practices and accurately simulating real-world conditions, you can identify and address performance issues before they impact your users, resulting in a smoother and more reliable user experience.

3.3.2. Benchmarking and Load Testing

Benchmarking and load testing are critical components of SQL performance testing, allowing you to assess how your database system performs under different levels of stress and concurrency. In this section, we will delve into the importance of benchmarking and load testing, the steps to perform them effectively, and tools that can aid in the process.

Why Benchmarking and Load Testing Matter:

Benchmarking and load testing provide valuable insights into your database system's behavior and performance characteristics. Here's why they matter:

1. Performance Baseline: Establishing a performance baseline helps you understand how your system performs under normal conditions.

2. Stress Testing: Load testing helps you identify how your system behaves when subjected to high levels of traffic, enabling you to uncover bottlenecks and potential issues.

3. Scalability Assessment: By gradually increasing the load, you can assess your system's scalability and determine its capacity to handle growing user demands.

4. Resource Utilization: These tests reveal how your system utilizes resources like CPU, memory, and disk I/O under various loads.

5. Response Time Analysis: You can measure response times for different queries and transactions, ensuring they meet acceptable thresholds.

Performing Benchmarking and Load Testing:

Follow these steps to implement benchmarking and load testing effectively:

1. Define Test Scenarios: Identify the specific scenarios you want to test, such as user registration, data retrieval, or complex queries. Define realistic use cases.

2. Select Load Testing Tools: Choose a suitable load testing tool like Apache JMeter, Gatling, or Locust. These tools allow you to simulate multiple users and requests.

3. Create Test Scripts: Develop test scripts that mimic user interactions. These scripts should include a mix of read and write operations, as well as different user flows.

4. Set Load Levels: Gradually increase the load levels from a small number of concurrent users to simulate real-world traffic growth. Monitor performance at each level.

5. Monitor Resource Utilization: Use monitoring tools to track resource utilization during testing. Keep an eye on CPU, memory, disk I/O, and network bandwidth.

6. Measure Response Times: Record response times for different operations. Identify any queries or transactions that exceed predefined response time thresholds.

7. Analyze Bottlenecks: Utilize profiling and monitoring tools to identify performance bottlenecks. Common issues include slow queries, inefficient indexing, and resource contention.

8. Identify Breaking Points: Determine the maximum load your system can handle before performance degrades significantly. This helps in capacity planning.

9. Implement Test Automation: Automate your load tests so that they can be run regularly to monitor system performance over time.

Popular Load Testing Tools:

Here are a few load testing tools commonly used in the industry:

1. Apache JMeter: An open-source tool that allows you to create and run load tests on web applications, databases, and more.

2. Gatling: A highly scalable and performance-oriented load testing tool that uses a domain-specific language for test scripting.

3. Locust: An open-source Python-based load testing tool that focuses on simplicity and ease of use.

4. LoadRunner: A tool by Micro Focus that offers a wide range of load testing capabilities and supports various protocols and technologies.

5. K6: An open-source load testing tool that specializes in scripting for modern web applications and APIs.

Interpreting Load Test Results:

Once you've conducted benchmarking and load testing, analyze the results carefully. Look for:

1. Response Times: Ensure that response times for critical operations remain within acceptable limits. Identify outliers.

2. Throughput: Measure the number of requests your system can handle per second.

3. Resource Utilization: Check how system resources like CPU, memory, and disk I/O are used under load.

4. Error Rates: Monitor for increased error rates as load increases, which can indicate issues.

5. Scalability: Assess whether your system scales linearly or if there are diminishing returns beyond a certain point.

6. Bottlenecks: Identify performance bottlenecks and address them through optimizations.

In conclusion, benchmarking and load testing are indispensable for evaluating your database system's performance. By simulating real-world scenarios and progressively increasing loads, you can uncover weaknesses, fine-tune your system, and ensure it meets the demands of your users. Regular testing and monitoring are key to maintaining optimal database performance over time.

3.3.3. Analyzing Test Results

Analyzing test results is a crucial step in the SQL performance testing process. It provides insights into how your database system performs under different conditions and helps you identify performance bottlenecks, optimizations, and potential issues. In this section, we will explore the significance of analyzing test results, the steps to perform a comprehensive analysis, and how to interpret the findings.

Why Analyzing Test Results Matters:

Analyzing test results is essential for several reasons:

1. Performance Validation: It verifies whether your database system meets the performance requirements and goals you defined earlier.

2. Bottleneck Identification: It helps identify performance bottlenecks, such as slow queries, resource constraints, or contention issues.

3. Optimization Insights: Analysis reveals areas that require optimization, enabling you to make data-driven decisions on performance improvements.

4. Resource Utilization: You can assess how system resources like CPU, memory, and storage are utilized during testing.

5. Scaling Assessment: It determines how well your system scales with increased load and user concurrency.

6. Error Detection: Analysis helps spot errors, exceptions, or anomalies that may occur during testing.

Steps to Analyze Test Results:

Here's a step-by-step guide on how to analyze SQL performance test results effectively:

Step 1: Collect Test Data

Before analysis, ensure you have collected comprehensive test data. This data should include metrics like response times, throughput, resource utilization, and error rates. Test data should be organized and easily accessible.

Step 2: Define Key Metrics

Identify the key performance metrics you want to focus on during analysis. Common metrics include average response time, 90th percentile response time, error rate, throughput, and resource usage (CPU, memory, disk I/O).

Step 3: Create Visualizations

Visualizations are powerful tools for understanding your test results. Create graphs, charts, and dashboards to visualize performance trends and variations over time. Use tools like Grafana, Kibana, or built-in reporting features in load testing tools.

Step 4: Compare Baseline and Load Test Data

Compare the performance metrics of your baseline test (normal operating conditions) with the load test results. This comparison helps you understand how your system behaves under different loads.

Step 5: Identify Performance Bottlenecks

Look for bottlenecks in your system. These could be slow SQL queries, inefficient indexing, contention for resources, or any other factor that negatively impacts performance. Profiling and monitoring tools can help pinpoint bottlenecks.

Step 6: Analyze Resource Utilization

Examine how system resources are utilized during testing. High CPU or memory usage may indicate resource bottlenecks, while excessive disk I/O could point to storage-related issues.

Step 7: Investigate Error Rates

Check error rates during load testing. Elevated error rates may indicate issues with your application, database, or network connectivity. Investigate and address these errors.

Step 8: Assess Scalability

Evaluate how well your system scales. Determine whether performance scales linearly with increased load or if there are diminishing returns. This assessment helps in capacity planning.

Step 9: Prioritize Optimizations

Based on your findings, prioritize optimizations. Consider database schema changes, query optimizations, indexing improvements, or resource upgrades to address bottlenecks and performance issues.

Step 10: Document Findings

Document your analysis findings, including identified bottlenecks and proposed optimizations. Use this documentation as a reference for implementing improvements and tracking progress.

Interpreting Analysis Findings:

Interpreting analysis findings requires a deep understanding of your application, database, and system architecture. Here are some common interpretations:

1. Slow Queries: Slow queries may indicate the need for query optimization, better indexing, or caching strategies.

2. Resource Bottlenecks: High CPU, memory, or disk usage may require scaling resources or optimizing code that consumes these resources.

3. Concurrency Issues: Contention for resources like locks or connections can lead to performance degradation and require careful management.

4. Scalability Limits: Identifying when performance plateaus under increased load helps in capacity planning and resource allocation.

5. Error Patterns: Consistently high error rates may point to application bugs, database configuration issues, or network problems.

6. Regression Testing: After implementing optimizations, perform regression testing to confirm that changes have a positive impact on performance.

In conclusion, analyzing SQL performance test results is essential for ensuring your database system meets performance requirements. It helps you identify bottlenecks, optimize queries, and fine-tune your system for optimal performance. Regular analysis and monitoring are key to maintaining a high-performing database over time.

PART IV
In-Depth SQL Performance Tuning Strategies

4.1 Index Tuning for Databases

4.1.1. Understanding Different Types of Indexes

Index tuning is a critical aspect of SQL performance optimization. Indexes are database structures that enhance query performance by allowing the database engine to quickly locate and retrieve rows from a table. In this section, we will delve into the world of indexes, exploring various types of indexes and understanding when and how to use them for optimal SQL performance.

Why Understanding Indexes Matters:

Indexes play a pivotal role in optimizing SQL queries. They provide faster data retrieval by creating a structured path to data rows. Understanding indexes is crucial because:

1. Improved Query Performance: Well-designed indexes can significantly reduce query execution times, making your applications more responsive.

2. Reduced Resource Usage: Efficient index usage consumes fewer server resources, such as CPU and memory, leading to better overall system performance.

3. Faster Sorting and Joining: Indexes speed up sorting and joining operations, which are common in SQL queries involving multiple tables.

4. Enhanced Concurrency: Properly indexed tables can support higher levels of concurrent users without compromising performance.

5. Better Data Integrity: Indexes can enforce data integrity constraints like unique and primary keys.

Types of Indexes:

There are several types of indexes available in most relational database management systems (RDBMS). Let's explore the most common ones:

1. B-Tree Indexes:

- **Description:** B-tree (balanced tree) indexes are the most common type of index. They are well-suited for columns with high cardinality (many distinct values) and are efficient for equality and range queries.

- **Use Cases:** Use B-tree indexes for primary keys, foreign keys, and columns frequently used in WHERE clauses with equality operators (e.g., =, <>, IN).

2. Bitmap Indexes:

- **Description:** Bitmap indexes use a bitmap for each distinct value in the indexed column. They are excellent for low cardinality columns (few distinct values) and work well with columns that have boolean or categorical data.

- **Use Cases:** Consider bitmap indexes for columns with low cardinality, such as gender or boolean flags, as well as for complex queries involving multiple conditions.

3. Hash Indexes:

- **Description:** Hash indexes are suitable for exact match queries but not for range queries. They are particularly efficient when the indexed column contains data with a uniform distribution.

- Use Cases: Use hash indexes for columns with a uniform distribution and where exact match queries are predominant.

4. Full-Text Indexes:

- Description: Full-text indexes are designed for searching text data efficiently. They enable searching for words or phrases within text columns and support advanced text search capabilities.

- Use Cases: Implement full-text indexes for columns containing large text bodies, such as articles, comments, or product descriptions.

5. Spatial Indexes:

- Description: Spatial indexes are specialized for geographic data and support spatial queries like finding nearby locations, determining distances, and performing geometry-based operations.

- Use Cases: Utilize spatial indexes when dealing with geographic data, such as mapping applications, GPS coordinates, or spatial analysis.

6. Clustered and Non-Clustered Indexes:

- Description: Clustered indexes determine the physical order of rows in a table, whereas non-clustered indexes provide an alternative logical order. A table can have only one clustered index but multiple non-clustered indexes.

- Use Cases: Clustered indexes are often used for primary keys, while non-clustered indexes can improve the performance of frequently queried columns.

7. Covering Indexes:

- Description: A covering index includes all the columns needed to satisfy a query, eliminating the need for additional lookups in the base table. They are valuable for query performance optimization.

- Use Cases: Create covering indexes for queries with specific column selections, as they reduce the I/O and CPU overhead of lookups.

When and How to Use Indexes:

While indexes offer significant benefits, they come with trade-offs in terms of storage and maintenance overhead. Here's a step-by-step guide on when and how to use indexes effectively:

Step 1: Identify Query Patterns:

- Analyze your application's query patterns to determine which columns are frequently used in WHERE clauses for filtering and JOIN conditions.

Step 2: Prioritize Queries:

- Prioritize queries based on their impact on overall system performance. Focus on optimizing the most critical and frequently executed queries first.

Step 3: Create Indexes Carefully:

- Create indexes on columns used in WHERE clauses with equality operators or range queries. Avoid over-indexing, which can lead to performance degradation during data modification operations (INSERT, UPDATE, DELETE).

Step 4: Monitor Index Usage:

- Regularly monitor index usage and query performance. Unused or redundant indexes should be evaluated and potentially removed.

Step 5: Index Maintenance:

- Schedule regular index maintenance to rebuild or reorganize indexes. This prevents index fragmentation and ensures optimal query performance.

Step 6: Test and Iterate:

- Test the impact of index changes in a controlled environment. Monitor query execution plans and performance metrics. Iterate on your index design as needed.

Conclusion:

Understanding different types of indexes and when to use them is fundamental to SQL performance tuning. Well-designed indexes can significantly boost query performance, while poorly designed ones can lead to inefficiencies and increased resource consumption. When used judiciously and maintained properly, indexes are a powerful tool in your SQL optimization toolbox.

4.1.2. Indexing Best Practices

Indexing is a critical aspect of database performance tuning. When done correctly, indexing can dramatically improve query response times and overall system efficiency. In this section, we will delve into best practices for designing and managing indexes in your database.

Why Indexing Best Practices Matter:

Effective indexing is crucial for the following reasons:

1. Enhanced Query Performance: Well-designed indexes allow the database engine to locate and retrieve data quickly, resulting in faster query execution.

2. Reduced Resource Usage: Efficient index usage consumes fewer server resources, including CPU and memory, leading to better overall system performance.

3. Improved Data Integrity: Indexes can enforce data integrity constraints like unique keys, ensuring the accuracy and reliability of your data.

4. Optimized Sorting and Joining: Indexes are vital for optimizing sorting and joining operations, common in complex SQL queries.

5. Concurrency Support: Properly indexed tables can handle more concurrent users without compromising performance.

Indexing Best Practices:

To leverage the benefits of indexing and avoid common pitfalls, follow these best practices:

1. Identify High-Value Queries:

   - Start by identifying the queries that are critical to your application's performance. Focus on optimizing the queries with the most significant impact.

2. Prioritize Columns:

   - Not all columns require indexing. Prioritize columns based on their usage in WHERE clauses, JOIN conditions, and ORDER BY clauses.

3. Use the Right Type of Index:

   - Choose the appropriate index type for each column based on query patterns. Common index types include B-tree, bitmap, and full-text indexes.

4. Create Indexes Sparingly:

- Avoid over-indexing your tables, as each index consumes storage space and requires maintenance during data modifications (INSERT, UPDATE, DELETE). Indexes should provide a net benefit to query performance.

5. Follow Composite Index Guidelines:

- For queries involving multiple columns, consider creating composite indexes (indexes on multiple columns). Follow the order of columns in the index to match query conditions.

6. Utilize Filtered Indexes:

- Filtered indexes are indexes that include only a subset of rows in a table. Use them for queries with a specific WHERE clause condition to reduce index size and maintenance overhead.

7. Choose the Right Index Order:

- Pay attention to the order of columns in your indexes. It should match the query conditions and ORDER BY clauses. For example, for a query filtering by "A" and ordering by "B," create an index on (A, B).

8. Monitor Index Usage:

- Regularly monitor index usage and query performance. Identify unused or underutilized indexes and consider removing or optimizing them.

9. Beware of Index Fragmentation:

- Indexes can become fragmented over time due to data modifications. Schedule periodic index maintenance to rebuild or reorganize indexes and maintain their efficiency.

10. Know When to Defer Indexing:

- Consider deferring indexing for large initial data loads. Indexing during data import can slow down the process. Add indexes once the data is loaded.

11. Test Index Changes:

- Before implementing index changes in a production environment, thoroughly test them in a controlled setting. Monitor query execution plans and performance metrics to ensure improvements.

12. Document Indexing Decisions:

- Maintain documentation of index design decisions, including the rationale behind each index. This documentation helps with future maintenance and troubleshooting.

Indexing Best Practices in Action:

Let's walk through a practical example to illustrate these indexing best practices:

Scenario:

You are developing an e-commerce application with a product catalog database. One of your critical queries is to find all products in a specific category ordered by price. Here's how you can apply indexing best practices:

1. Identify High-Value Query: The query to retrieve products in a category ordered by price is a high-value query.

2. Prioritize Columns: In this query, the "category_id" column is used in the WHERE clause, and the "price" column is used in the ORDER BY clause. These columns should be prioritized for indexing.

3. Use the Right Type of Index: Consider using a B-tree index for "category_id" and "price" columns, as they are frequently used in equality and sorting operations.

4. Create Indexes Sparingly: Create indexes only on "category_id" and "price" columns to avoid unnecessary overhead.

5. Follow Composite Index Guidelines: Since the query filters by "category_id" and orders by "price," create a composite index on (category_id, price).

6. Utilize Filtered Indexes: If there are subcategories within the "category_id" and the query often filters for a specific subcategory, consider creating a filtered index on (category_id) WHERE subcategory = 'specific_subcategory'.

7. Choose the Right Index Order: Ensure that the composite index order matches the query conditions (category_id, price).

8. Monitor Index Usage: Regularly monitor query performance and index usage. If a new query pattern emerges, consider adjusting indexes accordingly.

9. Beware of Index Fragmentation: Schedule periodic index maintenance to manage fragmentation, especially if the product catalog experiences frequent updates.

10. Know When to Defer Indexing: During the initial product catalog data import, defer index creation to expedite the import process.

11. Test Index Changes: Before deploying to production, test the indexing changes on a similar-sized dataset to validate performance improvements.

12. Document Indexing Decisions: Maintain documentation detailing the indexes created, their purpose, and their expected impact on query performance.

By following these indexing best practices, you can optimize the performance of critical queries in your database while minimizing maintenance overhead. Effective indexing is an essential skill for any database administrator or developer aiming to deliver high-performance database-driven applications.

4.1.3. Handling Index Fragmentation

Index fragmentation is a common issue that can degrade the performance of your database over time. When data is added, updated, or deleted in your tables, it can lead to fragmentation in the associated indexes. In this section, we will explore what index fragmentation is, why it's a problem, and how to handle it effectively.

Understanding Index Fragmentation:

Index fragmentation occurs when the logical order of index pages doesn't match the physical order of data pages in your database. There are two main types of index fragmentation:

1. Internal Fragmentation: This type of fragmentation occurs when there are gaps between the pages of an index. It happens due to page splits caused by INSERT or UPDATE operations.

2. External Fragmentation: External fragmentation refers to the physical disorganization of index pages on disk. It occurs when index pages are not stored sequentially, leading to additional disk I/O operations.

Why Index Fragmentation Matters:

Index fragmentation can significantly impact database performance for several reasons:

1. Slower Query Execution: Fragmented indexes require more disk I/O to read data, leading to slower query execution times.

2. Increased Storage Requirements: Fragmented indexes consume more disk space than well-organized ones.

3. Higher Maintenance Overhead: SQL Server must perform additional maintenance tasks, such as index reorganization or rebuilds, to manage fragmentation.

Handling Index Fragmentation:

To mitigate the negative effects of index fragmentation, follow these steps:

1. Regular Index Maintenance:

  - Schedule regular index maintenance tasks to address fragmentation issues. Two common methods are index reorganization and index rebuild.

2. Index Reorganization:

  - Index reorganization is a lightweight operation that defragments indexes by reordering index pages without requiring additional disk space. It is suitable for mildly fragmented indexes (less than 30% fragmentation).

3. Index Rebuild:

  - Index rebuild recreates the entire index, eliminating fragmentation entirely. It requires more disk space and can be a resource-intensive operation. Use it for heavily fragmented indexes (greater than 30% fragmentation).

4. Fragmentation Analysis:

- Use built-in database management tools to monitor and analyze index fragmentation levels. SQL Server Management Studio (SSMS) provides reports and scripts for this purpose.

5. Scheduled Maintenance Plans:

- Consider creating scheduled maintenance plans or SQL Server Agent jobs to automate index maintenance tasks.

6. Prioritize Critical Indexes:

- Focus on defragmenting indexes that are critical for query performance. Identify high-fragmentation indexes using fragmentation reports.

7. Keep Statistics Updated:

- Ensure that statistics are up-to-date, as they play a crucial role in query optimization and execution plans.

8. Disk Management:

- Maintain sufficient free space on your storage devices to accommodate index rebuilds when needed.

Example:

Let's walk through an example of handling index fragmentation:

Scenario:

You have a SQL Server database used for an e-commerce website. The "Orders" table has a clustered index on the "OrderID" column. Over time, this index has become fragmented due to frequent order updates and insertions.

Steps to Handle Index Fragmentation:

1. Identify Fragmented Index: Use SSMS or the following T-SQL query to identify the fragmentation level of the clustered index:

```sql
SELECT OBJECT_NAME(IX.OBJECT_ID) AS TableName,
    IX.NAME AS IndexName,
    PS.[avg_fragmentation_in_percent]
FROM sys.dm_db_index_physical_stats(DB_ID(), NULL, NULL, NULL, NULL) AS PS
INNER JOIN sys.indexes AS IX ON PS.[object_id] = IX.[object_id]
            AND PS.[index_id] = IX.[index_id]
WHERE OBJECT_NAME(IX.OBJECT_ID) = 'Orders';
```

2. Determine the Level of Fragmentation: Based on the query result, if the fragmentation level is above 30%, consider rebuilding the index.

3. Schedule Index Maintenance: Create a SQL Server Agent job or maintenance plan to run index rebuild or reorganize tasks regularly. For the "Orders" table, you might choose to rebuild the clustered index monthly.

4. Monitor and Adjust: Periodically monitor index fragmentation levels and adjust your maintenance schedule as needed.

By addressing index fragmentation, you can ensure that your database maintains optimal performance over time. Regular maintenance helps prevent performance degradation and ensures that your database continues to deliver efficient query execution.

4.2 Optimizing SQL Statements

4.2.1. Advanced Query Optimization Techniques

Query optimization is a critical aspect of SQL performance tuning. In this section, we will explore advanced techniques to optimize SQL queries for better performance. These techniques go beyond the basics and are particularly useful when dealing with complex queries or large datasets.

1. Understanding Query Execution Plans:

   - Query execution plans are the roadmaps that SQL Server uses to execute SQL queries. Understanding these plans is crucial for query optimization. You can obtain execution plans using tools like SQL Server Management Studio (SSMS) or by enabling the "Include Actual Execution Plan" option in your query window.

2. Indexing Strategies:

   - Proper indexing is fundamental to query optimization. Advanced indexing techniques include:

   - **Covering Indexes:** These indexes cover all the columns required for a query, reducing the need to access the actual data rows.

   - **Filtered Indexes:** Use filtered indexes to index a subset of rows in a table, which can be beneficial for queries that target specific criteria.

   - **Indexed Views:** Consider creating indexed views for complex queries that involve aggregations or joins.

3. Query Rewrite and Transformation:

- Advanced query optimization often involves rewriting or transforming queries to make them more efficient. Techniques include:

- **Subquery Unnesting:** Convert correlated subqueries into joins for better performance.

- **Common Table Expressions (CTEs):** Use CTEs to simplify complex queries and improve readability.

- **Window Functions:** Leverage window functions like ROW_NUMBER(), RANK(), and DENSE_RANK() to perform advanced analytics within a query.

4. Query Hints and Plan Guides:

- Sometimes, you may need to override the query optimizer's decisions. You can achieve this with query hints or plan guides. Common hints include:

- **OPTION (RECOMPILE):** Forces SQL Server to recompile the query plan each time it's executed, which can adapt to changing data.

- **OPTION (HASH JOIN):** Specifies that a hash join should be used instead of the default join method.

5. Parallel Query Execution:

- SQL Server can execute queries in parallel, which can significantly boost performance for CPU-bound queries. Use the MAXDOP (Maximum Degree of Parallelism) query hint to control parallelism.

6. Tempdb Optimization:

- Tempdb is a crucial system database that can affect query performance. Optimize tempdb by:

- Properly sizing tempdb files based on your workload.

- Isolating tempdb onto dedicated storage for better I/O performance.

7. Query Performance Analysis:

- Tools like SQL Server Profiler and Extended Events allow you to capture and analyze query performance. Monitor query execution times, reads, writes, and other relevant metrics.

8. Plan Caching:

- SQL Server caches query plans to reuse them when the same query is executed again. However, plan caching can sometimes lead to performance issues. Techniques to manage plan caching include:

  - Plan freezing: Prevents query plan changes for a specific query.

  - Forced plan: Enforces a particular query plan for a query.

9. Resource Governor:

- Use SQL Server's Resource Governor to allocate resources based on workload priorities. This ensures that critical queries get the necessary resources for optimal performance.

Example: Advanced Query Optimization

Let's consider an example where you have a large e-commerce database, and you want to optimize a complex query that retrieves sales data for the past year, grouped by product category and customer location. The query takes too long to execute.

Steps to Optimize the Query:

1. Review the Execution Plan:

- Analyze the execution plan to identify potential bottlenecks. Look for missing indexes or expensive operators like table scans or sorts.

2. Index Optimization:

- Create covering indexes for the involved tables, including the sales, products, and customers tables. Ensure that these indexes cover the columns in your query's SELECT, WHERE, and JOIN clauses.

3. Subquery to Join Conversion:

- Rewrite subqueries as JOINs to reduce correlated subquery performance overhead.

4. Use CTEs:

- Implement Common Table Expressions (CTEs) to break down complex queries into more manageable parts.

5. Tempdb Optimization:

- Optimize tempdb by sizing it appropriately and placing it on fast storage.

6. Monitor Query Performance:

- Use SQL Server Profiler to capture and analyze query execution times and resource usage. Adjust your query optimization strategy based on these metrics.

By applying these advanced query optimization techniques, you can significantly improve the performance of complex SQL queries and ensure that your database operates efficiently, even with large datasets and complex queries.

4.2.2. Using Hints and Optimizer Overrides

In the world of SQL query optimization, sometimes you need to take matters into your own hands. SQL query hints and optimizer overrides are advanced techniques that allow you to exert more control over how the database engine executes your queries. While they should be used judiciously, they can be powerful tools for achieving optimal query performance in specific scenarios.

Understanding Query Hints and Optimizer Overrides:

Query hints and optimizer overrides are directives given to the database engine to influence the query execution plan. They provide instructions on how to retrieve data, which indexes to use, and even the join methods to employ. While these hints can be invaluable for fine-tuning query performance, they should be used with caution, as they can lead to suboptimal plans if misapplied.

Common Query Hints and Optimizer Overrides:

1. OPTION (RECOMPILE): The `OPTION (RECOMPILE)` hint forces the database engine to recompile the query plan every time it's executed. This can be beneficial when query parameters vary significantly and you want to ensure the plan adapts to changing data distributions.

- **Example:**

```sql
SELECT * FROM Orders WHERE OrderDate > '2023-01-01' OPTION (RECOMPILE);
```

2. OPTION (HASH JOIN): The `OPTION (HASH JOIN)` hint instructs the optimizer to use a hash join instead of the default join method. Hash joins can be advantageous for large tables or non-indexed columns.

- **Example:**

```sql
SELECT * FROM Customers c

JOIN Orders o ON c.CustomerID = o.CustomerID

OPTION (HASH JOIN);
```

3. FORCESEEK: The `FORCESEEK` hint encourages the database engine to use an index seek operation instead of a scan. This can be useful when you know that an index provides faster access to the required data.

- **Example:**

```sql
SELECT * FROM Products WITH (FORCESEEK(IndexName)) WHERE Category = 'Electronics';
```

4. OPTIMIZE FOR: The `OPTIMIZE FOR` hint allows you to optimize a query for specific parameter values. It can help create a more efficient plan when you know common parameter values used in practice.

- **Example:**

```sql
```

SELECT * FROM Customers WHERE Country = @Country

OPTION (OPTIMIZE FOR (@Country = 'USA'));

```

**5. KEEPPLAN:** The `KEEPPLAN` hint suggests to the optimizer that it should retain the existing query plan in the plan cache, even if it believes a recompile is necessary. This can be used to ensure plan stability in certain scenarios.

   **- Example:**

   ```sql

   SELECT * FROM Products WHERE Category = 'Clothing'

   OPTION (KEEPPLAN);

   ```

6. QUERYTRACEON: The `QUERYTRACEON` hint activates a specific trace flag for the duration of the query. Trace flags are used for debugging and optimization purposes. Use this hint with caution and refer to official documentation for valid trace flag values.

   - Example:

   ```sql

   SELECT * FROM Employees

   OPTION (QUERYTRACEON 9481);

   ```

Guidelines for Using Hints and Optimizer Overrides:
   ```

While query hints and optimizer overrides can be powerful tools, here are some guidelines to follow:

1. Start with Proper Indexing: Before resorting to hints, ensure your tables are well-indexed. The optimizer can make better decisions with the right indexes in place.

2. Profile and Analyze: Use performance profiling tools to identify query bottlenecks. Only apply hints where necessary based on empirical evidence.

3. Limit Their Use: Avoid overusing hints, as they can make queries less adaptable to changing data or system configurations.

4. Test Thoroughly: Before deploying hints to production, thoroughly test their impact on query performance across different scenarios and data distributions.

5. Document Extensively: Keep detailed documentation of where and why you've applied hints to queries, as this will aid troubleshooting and future optimizations.

Example: Applying a Query Hint

Suppose you have a query that retrieves the top 10 highest-priced products from your inventory table. You've noticed that the optimizer sometimes chooses a suboptimal execution plan, resulting in slower query performance.

```sql
SELECT TOP 10 * FROM Products ORDER BY Price DESC;
```

You decide to apply a query hint to force the use of an index seek operation on the Price column, as you know that it provides better performance for this query.

```sql
SELECT TOP 10 * FROM Products WITH (FORCESEEK(IX_Price)) ORDER BY Price DESC;
```

By using the `WITH (FORCESEEK(IX_Price))` hint, you guide the optimizer to use the specified index (`IX_Price`) to perform an index seek, ensuring faster retrieval of the top-priced products.

In conclusion, query hints and optimizer overrides are advanced tools that can help fine-tune query performance when used judiciously. However, they should be employed based on empirical evidence and careful testing to ensure they genuinely improve query execution plans.

4.2.3. Managing Temporary Tables and Memory Usage

Optimizing SQL statements often involves more than just crafting efficient queries; it also requires managing temporary tables and memory usage effectively. Temporary tables play a crucial role in many database operations, from complex joins to intermediate result sets. In this section, we'll explore strategies for optimizing temporary tables and memory usage to enhance SQL query performance.

Understanding Temporary Tables:

Temporary tables are a powerful database feature used to store intermediate results during query execution. They are particularly useful when dealing with complex joins, aggregations, or data transformations. Temporary tables are temporary in nature, meaning they are automatically dropped when the session or transaction ends, making them ideal for intermediate storage.

Common Use Cases for Temporary Tables:

1. Intermediate Result Sets: When a query involves multiple joins or complex calculations, temporary tables can store interim results, reducing the complexity of the main query.

2. Data Transformation: Temporary tables are valuable for transforming data, such as pivoting, aggregating, or applying business logic, before incorporating it into the final result.

3. Complex Reporting: In reporting scenarios, temporary tables can help precompute and organize data for faster reporting generation.

Optimizing Temporary Tables and Memory Usage:

To ensure temporary tables don't become a performance bottleneck, consider the following strategies:

1. Indexing Temporary Tables: Just like regular tables, temporary tables can benefit from proper indexing. Analyze query execution plans to identify which columns are frequently used in joins or filtering, and index those columns to improve performance.

- **Example:**

```sql
CREATE CLUSTERED INDEX IX_TempTable_Column1 ON #TempTable(Column1);
```

2. Limit Data Size: Be cautious about the volume of data stored in temporary tables. Retrieve only the necessary columns and rows to reduce memory and disk I/O overhead.

- Example:

```sql
INSERT INTO #TempTable (Column1, Column2)

SELECT Column1, Column2

FROM LargeTable

WHERE Condition = 'Filtered';
```

3. Proper Memory Configuration: Ensure that your database server has sufficient memory available for temporary tables. Configuring the right amount of memory for sorting and hashing operations can significantly impact query performance.

4. Use Table Variables When Appropriate: In some cases, using table variables (`DECLARE @TableVariable`) instead of temporary tables (`#TempTable`) can improve performance. Table variables are stored in memory and are suitable for smaller datasets.

- Example:

```sql
DECLARE @TableVariable TABLE (Column1 INT, Column2 VARCHAR(50));

INSERT INTO @TableVariable (Column1, Column2) VALUES (1, 'Value1');
```

5. Drop Temporary Tables Promptly: Temporary tables are automatically dropped at the end of a session or transaction, but if they are no longer needed within a session, consider explicitly dropping them to free up resources.

- Example:

```sql
DROP TABLE #TempTable;
```

Example: Optimizing Temporary Table Usage

Let's consider an example where you have a complex reporting query that involves joining multiple large tables and aggregating data. To optimize this query, you decide to use a temporary table to store intermediate results.

```sql
-- Create a temporary table to store intermediate results
CREATE TABLE #IntermediateResults (
    ProductCategory VARCHAR(50),
    TotalSales DECIMAL(18, 2)
);


-- Insert aggregated data into the temporary table
INSERT INTO #IntermediateResults (ProductCategory, TotalSales)
SELECT ProductCategory, SUM(SalesAmount) AS TotalSales
FROM Sales
GROUP BY ProductCategory;


-- Retrieve the final report data from the temporary table
```

```sql
SELECT * FROM #IntermediateResults;


-- Drop the temporary table when no longer needed

DROP TABLE #IntermediateResults;
```

In this example, the temporary table `#IntermediateResults` is used to store aggregated data, reducing the complexity of the final query. Proper indexing and limiting data size in the temporary table can further enhance query performance.

Conclusion:

Optimizing SQL statements involves not only crafting efficient queries but also managing temporary tables and memory usage effectively. Temporary tables are valuable for storing intermediate results, but they should be used judiciously and optimized to ensure they contribute positively to query performance. By following best practices and monitoring resource utilization, you can achieve significant improvements in SQL query performance.

4.3 Tuning Database Connections

4.3.1. Connection Pooling and Management

Efficient management of database connections is a critical aspect of SQL performance tuning. In high-demand environments, improper connection handling can lead to performance bottlenecks and resource exhaustion. This section explores the importance of connection pooling and effective management techniques to optimize SQL query performance.

Understanding Database Connections:

Database connections are essential for applications to interact with databases. Each connection represents a communication pathway between an application and the database server. Establishing and maintaining connections consume server resources, and excessive connections can lead to server overload and degraded performance.

Challenges with Connection Management:

Inefficient connection management can result in several challenges:

1. Resource Consumption: Each open connection consumes server memory and other resources. A surge in connections can lead to resource exhaustion and slow down the database server.

2. Latency: Establishing new connections incurs latency. If connections are constantly opened and closed, it can significantly impact query response times.

3. Contention: High contention for connections can lead to contention-related bottlenecks, causing queries to queue up and wait for available connections.

Connection Pooling:

Connection pooling is a technique that mitigates these challenges by reusing existing connections instead of creating new ones for each user request. A connection pool maintains a pool of open connections that applications can reuse, reducing the overhead of connection establishment and teardown.

Configuring Connection Pools:

Configuring connection pools is database-specific, but here's a general outline of the process:

1. Specify Pool Size: Determine the appropriate number of connections to maintain in the pool based on your application's expected load. Too few connections can lead to contention, while too many can waste resources.

  - Example: Configuring a Connection Pool in Java with Apache DBCP:

```java
BasicDataSource dataSource = new BasicDataSource();

dataSource.setDriverClassName("com.mysql.jdbc.Driver");

dataSource.setUrl("jdbc:mysql://localhost/mydb");

dataSource.setUsername("username");

dataSource.setPassword("password");

dataSource.setInitialSize(10); // Initial pool size

dataSource.setMaxTotal(50);    // Maximum pool size
```

2. Set Timeout Values: Define timeout settings to handle scenarios where all connections are in use. Timeouts ensure that applications don't hang indefinitely while waiting for a connection.

  - Example: Setting a Connection Timeout in a .NET Application:

```csharp
SqlConnectionStringBuilder builder = new SqlConnectionStringBuilder();

builder.DataSource = "localhost";

builder.InitialCatalog = "mydb";

builder.UserID = "username";

builder.Password = "password";

builder.ConnectTimeout = 15; // Connection timeout in seconds
```

3. Implement Proper Error Handling: Handle exceptions that may occur when connections are used. Proper error handling ensures that connections are released back to the pool even in error scenarios.

  - Example: Error Handling in Python with psycopg2:

```python
import psycopg2

try:
    connection = psycopg2.connect(
        dbname="mydb", user="username", password="password", host="localhost"
    )
    # Perform database operations
except psycopg2.Error as e:
```

```
    print("Error:", e)
finally:
  if connection:
    connection.close()  # Ensure the connection is returned to the pool
```
```

**Monitoring and Tuning Connection Pools:**

Effective connection pool management doesn't end with configuration. Regular monitoring and tuning are essential to ensure optimal performance. Key aspects to monitor include:

**1. Connection Usage:** Keep track of the number of connections in use and the rate at which connections are borrowed and returned.

**2. Pool Size:** Ensure that the pool size aligns with your application's needs. Adjust it if you observe high contention or underutilization.

**3. Connection Leaks:** Detect and address connection leaks where connections are not properly closed and returned to the pool.

**4. Idle Connection Removal:** Consider implementing a mechanism to remove idle connections from the pool after a certain period to free up resources.

**Conclusion:**

Connection pooling and effective connection management are crucial elements of SQL performance tuning. By configuring connection pools, setting appropriate timeouts, and
```

implementing robust error handling, you can significantly improve application performance and resource utilization while interacting with databases. Regular monitoring and tuning ensure that your connection pool continues to meet the demands of your application efficiently.

4.3.2. Handling Deadlocks and Blocking

Database deadlocks and blocking are common issues that can severely impact application performance. In this section, we'll explore the concepts of deadlocks and blocking, their causes, and strategies to handle them effectively.

Understanding Deadlocks:

A deadlock occurs when two or more transactions are unable to proceed because they are each waiting for a resource that is held by another transaction in the deadlock. This situation leads to a standstill, where no transaction can progress, and the database server must resolve the deadlock.

Causes of Deadlocks:

Deadlocks typically occur due to the following conditions:

1. Resource Contention: Transactions are competing for resources, such as rows in a table, and each holds a resource that the other needs.

2. Circular Waiting: Transactions are waiting for each other in a circular manner. Transaction A is waiting for a resource held by B, B is waiting for C, and C is waiting for A.

Effects of Deadlocks:

Deadlocks can have severe consequences on database performance:

1. Blocking: Transactions involved in a deadlock are blocked, and their associated resources are locked, preventing other transactions from accessing them.

2. Increased Latency: Transactions waiting for deadlocked resources experience increased response times, leading to a degraded user experience.

3. Resource Wastage: Deadlocked transactions consume server resources while making no progress, wasting CPU and memory.

Strategies for Handling Deadlocks:

Effective deadlock handling involves prevention, detection, and resolution. Here are strategies to mitigate and manage deadlocks:

1. Lock Hierarchy: Implement a well-defined lock hierarchy to ensure that transactions always request locks in the same order. This minimizes the chances of circular waiting.

   - **Example:** If transactions need to access both table A and table B, ensure that they always request locks on these tables in the same order, such as A before B.

2. Lock Timeout: Set a timeout for transactions waiting for locks. If a transaction cannot acquire a lock within a specified time, it can be aborted or rolled back.

   - **Example:** In SQL Server, you can use the `SET LOCK_TIMEOUT` option to specify a timeout period for lock acquisition.

3. Deadlock Detection: Implement a deadlock detection mechanism that identifies and resolves deadlocks when they occur.

  - **Example:** In MySQL, you can enable the `innodb_deadlock_detect_interval` parameter to specify how often deadlock detection should be performed.

4. Transaction Retry: In case of a deadlock, applications can implement logic to retry the transaction. However, this should be done cautiously to avoid creating more deadlocks.

  - **Example:** In a Java application using JDBC, you can catch deadlock-related exceptions and retry the transaction a limited number of times.

Handling Blocking:

Blocking occurs when a transaction is waiting for a resource held by another transaction but is not part of a deadlock. While blocking is less severe than a deadlock, it can still impact performance.

Strategies for Handling Blocking:

1. Lock Timeout: As with deadlocks, setting a timeout for locks can help prevent long-term blocking situations.

  - **Example:** In Oracle, you can use the `WAIT` clause when requesting locks to specify the maximum time a transaction is willing to wait.

2. Optimistic Concurrency Control: Implement optimistic concurrency control, where transactions do not lock resources during read operations but check for conflicts before committing changes.

  - **Example:** In web applications, use version numbers or timestamps to track changes and detect conflicts during updates.

3. Monitor and Identify: Continuously monitor the database for blocking incidents and identify long-running or problematic queries.

  - **Example:** In SQL Server, you can use the `sys.dm_exec_requests` and `sys.dm_os_waiting_tasks` views to identify blocked and blocking queries.

Conclusion:

Handling deadlocks and blocking is crucial for maintaining a responsive and efficient database system. By implementing preventive measures, detecting incidents, and having effective resolution strategies in place, you can minimize the impact of these issues on your application's performance. Careful database design, transaction management, and monitoring are key to addressing deadlocks and blocking effectively.

4.3.3. Scaling Connection Handling

Scaling connection handling is a critical aspect of database performance tuning, especially in applications with high user concurrency. In this section, we'll explore strategies and techniques for efficiently managing database connections to ensure optimal performance as your application grows.

Understanding Connection Handling:

Database connections are a finite and valuable resource. Each active connection consumes memory, CPU, and other server resources. When the number of concurrent connections exceeds the server's capacity, performance bottlenecks and resource exhaustion can occur.

Challenges in Scaling Connection Handling:

Scaling connection handling involves addressing several challenges:

1. Resource Utilization: Efficiently utilizing available database resources (CPU, memory, disk) to handle a growing number of connections.

2. Concurrency: Allowing multiple users to simultaneously interact with the database while maintaining data consistency.

3. Connection Pooling: Managing a pool of reusable connections to minimize the overhead of creating and destroying connections for each user.

Strategies for Scaling Connection Handling:

Here are strategies and best practices to efficiently scale connection handling:

1. Connection Pooling:

   - **What:** Connection pooling involves maintaining a pool of established database connections that can be reused by multiple client applications.

- **Why:** Creating and destroying connections for each user is resource-intensive. Connection pooling minimizes this overhead.

- **How:** Most database drivers and application frameworks offer built-in connection pooling mechanisms. Configure the pool size, connection timeout, and idle connection handling.

- **Example (Java - JDBC):** Use a connection pool library like Apache DBCP or HikariCP. Set parameters like `maxPoolSize` to control the number of connections.

2. Resource Management:

- **What:** Monitor and manage server resources (CPU, memory, disk) to ensure they are sufficient to handle the expected number of connections.

- **Why:** Overloading server resources can lead to performance degradation and resource contention.

- **How:** Use server monitoring tools to track resource utilization. Allocate additional resources as needed.

- **Example:** In a cloud-based environment, you can vertically scale by increasing the instance size or horizontally scale by adding more database replicas.

3. Connection Limits:

- **What:** Enforce connection limits or quotas for users or applications based on their requirements.

- **Why:** Preventing users or applications from monopolizing resources ensures fair resource allocation.

- **How:** Set maximum connection limits in your database management system or application server.

- **Example (MySQL):** Use the `max_connections` configuration to limit the total number of concurrent connections.

4. Connection Idle Timeout:

- **What:** Implement an idle timeout for database connections to release resources when connections are not in use.

- **Why:** Idle connections consume resources without serving any active queries.

- **How:** Configure an idle timeout value for connections in your connection pool settings.

- **Example (Oracle - SQL Developer):** Set the `Inactive Connection Timeout` option to automatically close idle connections.

5. Load Balancing:

- **What:** Distribute incoming database connection requests across multiple database servers.

- **Why:** Load balancing improves fault tolerance and scalability by distributing connections evenly.

- **How:** Use a load balancer or a database proxy that supports connection routing and load distribution.

- **Example:** Amazon RDS provides built-in load balancing for read-intensive workloads.

6. Connection Recycling:

- **What:** Reuse existing connections when possible rather than creating new ones.

- **Why:** Recycling connections reduces the overhead of establishing a new connection for each request.

- **How:** Design your application to check for and reuse existing connections before creating new ones.

- **Example (Python - SQLAlchemy):** Use the `pool_pre_ping` option to enable connection recycling.

7. Asynchronous Processing:

- **What:** Implement asynchronous database access to minimize connection blocking and waiting.

- **Why:** Asynchronous operations allow other tasks to continue while database queries are in progress.

- How: Use programming frameworks that support asynchronous I/O or non-blocking database drivers.

- Example (Node.js - Node-oracledb): Utilize the asynchronous capabilities of Node.js to perform non-blocking database queries.

8. Session Management:

- What: Implement session management techniques to reduce the number of active connections for each user.

- Why: Long-lived sessions with many open connections can strain database resources.

- How: Encourage users to close connections when they are done or implement session timeout mechanisms.

- Example: Educate developers to explicitly close connections after use in application code.

Conclusion:

Efficiently scaling connection handling is essential for maintaining database performance as your application grows. Connection pooling, resource management, and other strategies help ensure that your database can handle a high level of concurrency while efficiently utilizing server

4.4 Efficient Storage Performance and I/O

4.4.1. Storage Architecture Considerations

Efficient storage performance and I/O optimization are vital for maintaining a high-performing database system. In this section, we'll delve into storage architecture considerations and best practices to enhance your SQL database's performance.

Understanding Storage Architecture:

Storage architecture refers to how data is stored, retrieved, and managed on physical and logical storage devices. Optimizing this architecture can significantly impact SQL database performance.

Challenges in Storage Performance:

Several challenges are associated with achieving optimal storage performance:

1. I/O Bottlenecks: Slow disk I/O can lead to query performance degradation and response time delays.

2. Data Fragmentation: Fragmented data storage can result in longer seek times and reduced I/O efficiency.

3. Disk Latency: High disk latency can be caused by various factors, including slow storage devices or contention.

Strategies for Storage Architecture Optimization:

Here are strategies and best practices for optimizing storage architecture and improving SQL database performance:

1. RAID Configuration:

- **What:** Redundant Array of Independent Disks (RAID) configurations, such as RAID 0, RAID 1, RAID 5, or RAID 10, can be used to distribute data across multiple disks.

- **Why:** RAID configurations provide redundancy, improve data reliability, and can enhance I/O performance.

- **How:** Choose an appropriate RAID level based on your performance and redundancy requirements. RAID 10, for example, combines mirroring and striping for improved performance and fault tolerance.

- **Example:** When setting up a database server, configure RAID 10 for the database storage to balance performance and fault tolerance.

2. Storage Tiering:

- **What:** Storage tiering involves using different types of storage media (e.g., SSDs, HDDs) based on data access patterns.

- **Why:** Frequently accessed data can be stored on high-speed SSDs, while less frequently accessed data can be stored on cheaper HDDs.

- **How:** Identify access patterns and categorize data into hot, warm, and cold tiers. Implement storage policies to automate tiering.

- **Example:** Use SQL Server's Storage Spaces feature to create storage tiers based on performance requirements.

3. Disk Partitioning:

- **What:** Divide physical storage into smaller partitions to segregate data and indexes.

- **Why:** Partitioning can improve I/O efficiency by allowing more granular control over data placement.

- **How:** Utilize the partitioning features provided by your database management system (DBMS). Partition tables based on criteria like date ranges or key values.

- **Example (Oracle):** Implement table partitioning in Oracle Database using the PARTITION BY clause.

4. Indexing Strategies:

- **What:** Properly index your database tables to speed up data retrieval.

- **Why:** Well-designed indexes can reduce the need for full table scans and improve query performance.

- **How:** Identify frequently queried columns and create appropriate indexes. Consider composite indexes for multi-column queries.

- **Example:** In a PostgreSQL database, create B-tree indexes on columns frequently used in WHERE clauses.

5. Filegroup Placement:

- **What:** Distribute database files (e.g., data files, log files) across multiple disks or disk arrays.

- **Why:** Distributing files can balance I/O load and reduce contention.

- **How:** When creating or expanding a database, specify different filegroups for different database objects and place them on separate disks.

- **Example:** In SQL Server, use filegroups to manage data file placement across multiple disks.

6. Monitor Disk Latency:

- **What:** Continuously monitor disk latency to identify and address performance bottlenecks.

- **Why:** Early detection of disk latency issues allows for timely intervention.

- **How:** Use database performance monitoring tools to track disk latency metrics. Set up alerts for thresholds.

- **Example:** Use tools like Microsoft Performance Monitor (PerfMon) or third-party monitoring solutions to track disk latency in real-time.

7. Regular Maintenance:

- **What:** Implement regular database maintenance tasks like defragmentation and index rebuilding.

- **Why:** Regular maintenance can help reduce data fragmentation and maintain optimal storage performance.

- **How:** Schedule maintenance tasks during low-traffic periods to minimize disruptions.

- **Example:** In SQL Server, use the Maintenance Plan Wizard to set up automated maintenance tasks.

8. Solid-State Drives (SSDs):

- **What:** Consider upgrading to SSDs for high-performance I/O.

- **Why:** SSDs offer significantly faster read/write speeds compared to traditional HDDs.

- **How:** Replace or supplement existing HDDs with SSDs for data storage.

- **Example:** When configuring a new database server, opt for SSDs as the primary storage medium.

Conclusion:

Efficient storage architecture is crucial for maintaining SQL database performance. By implementing these strategies and best practices, you can optimize your storage infrastructure to minimize I/O bottlenecks, reduce latency, and ensure your database operates at peak efficiency. Regular monitoring and proactive management are key to achieving and sustaining high-performance storage for your SQL database.

4.4.2. Reducing Disk I/O and Latency

Disk Input/Output (I/O) and latency are critical factors in SQL database performance. High I/O load and latency can lead to slow query execution and a poor user experience. In this section, we will explore strategies to reduce disk I/O and latency, ultimately improving your SQL database's performance.

Understanding Disk I/O and Latency:

Disk I/O refers to the process of reading and writing data to and from storage devices, such as hard drives or SSDs. Disk latency is the delay between a request for data and its retrieval. High I/O load and latency can occur due to factors like inefficient queries, lack of indexing, or disk hardware limitations.

Strategies to Reduce Disk I/O and Latency:

Let's dive into practical strategies for reducing disk I/O and latency in your SQL database:

1. Query Optimization:

- **What:** Optimize your SQL queries to retrieve only the necessary data. Use appropriate filtering conditions and limit result sets.

- **Why:** Efficient queries reduce the amount of data transferred between storage and memory.

- **How:** Review and analyze slow-performing queries. Use SQL profiling tools to identify bottlenecks. Rewrite or refactor queries for improved efficiency.

- **Example:** Consider a query that retrieves all columns from a table when only a few are needed. Modify the query to select only the required columns.

2. Indexing:

- **What:** Create and maintain appropriate indexes on columns used in WHERE clauses and JOIN conditions.

- **Why:** Well-designed indexes can significantly reduce the need for full table scans, thus decreasing I/O.

- **How:** Identify frequently queried columns and create indexes on them. Regularly monitor index fragmentation and rebuild indexes when necessary.

- **Example:** In a PostgreSQL database, create B-tree indexes on columns used in WHERE conditions.

3. Caching:

- **What:** Implement caching mechanisms to store frequently accessed data in memory.

- **Why:** Caching reduces the need for disk I/O by serving data from memory, which is faster than reading from disk.

- **How:** Use caching frameworks like Redis or Memcached to store and retrieve frequently accessed data. Configure appropriate cache expiration policies.

- **Example:** Cache the results of frequently used database queries or store frequently accessed web page content in memory.

4. Data Compression:

- **What:** Implement data compression to reduce the amount of data transferred between storage and memory.

- **Why:** Compressed data requires fewer I/O operations, leading to reduced disk I/O and latency.

- **How:** Use database-specific data compression features or file-level compression tools. Monitor the trade-off between compression and CPU usage.

- **Example:** In SQL Server, enable data compression at the table or index level to reduce storage requirements.

5. Load Balancing:

- **What:** Distribute read-heavy and write-heavy workloads across multiple database instances or replicas.

- **Why:** Load balancing ensures that no single database instance is overwhelmed with I/O requests.

- **How:** Implement a load balancer that evenly distributes incoming database requests. Use read replicas for read-intensive operations.

- **Example:** Set up a MySQL or PostgreSQL cluster with read replicas to distribute read queries across multiple nodes.

6. Solid-State Drives (SSDs):

- **What:** Consider upgrading your storage infrastructure to use SSDs instead of traditional HDDs.

- **Why:** SSDs offer significantly faster read and write speeds, reducing disk latency.

- **How:** Replace or supplement existing HDDs with SSDs for data storage.

- **Example:** When configuring a new database server, choose SSDs as the primary storage medium.

7. Monitor and Tune:

- **What:** Continuously monitor disk I/O and latency metrics to identify bottlenecks and performance issues.

- **Why:** Proactive monitoring allows for timely intervention and adjustments.

- **How:** Use database performance monitoring tools to track I/O and latency. Set up alerts for predefined thresholds.

- **Example:** Use tools like Microsoft Performance Monitor (PerfMon) or third-party monitoring solutions to track disk I/O and latency in real-time.

Conclusion:

Reducing disk I/O and latency is crucial for optimizing SQL database performance. By following these strategies, you can minimize the impact of disk operations on query execution, resulting in faster and more responsive database systems. Regular monitoring and proactive management are key to achieving and maintaining low disk I/O and latency levels, ensuring your SQL database operates at peak efficiency.

4.4.3. Utilizing Solid-State Drives (SSDs) for Performance Boost

In the world of database management and SQL performance tuning, achieving optimal storage performance and minimizing Input/Output (I/O) bottlenecks is paramount. Solid-State Drives (SSDs) have emerged as a game-changing technology in this realm, offering remarkable improvements in I/O speed and overall database performance compared to traditional Hard Disk Drives (HDDs). In this section, we will explore how to leverage SSDs to boost the performance of your SQL databases.

Understanding Solid-State Drives (SSDs):

SSDs are storage devices that use NAND-based flash memory to store data persistently. Unlike HDDs, which rely on spinning disks and mechanical read/write heads, SSDs have no moving parts. This fundamental difference results in several key advantages:

1. Speed: SSDs can read and write data at a significantly faster rate than HDDs. This is because there are no physical components that need to move into position to access data.

2. Low Latency: The absence of mechanical components virtually eliminates seek time, leading to low read and write latency.

3. Reliability: With no moving parts, SSDs are less prone to mechanical failure.

4. Energy Efficiency: SSDs consume less power than HDDs, which can lead to reduced operating costs in data centers.

Leveraging SSDs for SQL Database Performance:

Let's explore how to effectively utilize SSDs to boost SQL database performance:

1. Identify Workloads:

   - **What:** Understand your database workloads to determine which components benefit the most from SSDs.

   - **Why:** SSDs can be expensive, so it's essential to prioritize their use for workloads that will experience the most significant performance gains.

   - **How:** Use monitoring tools and query analysis to identify the most I/O-intensive operations. Common examples include transaction logs, tempdb, and frequently accessed tables or indexes.

2. Choose the Right SSDs:

   - **What:** Select SSDs that align with your specific database performance needs.

- **Why:** Not all SSDs are created equal. Consider factors like capacity, endurance, and read/write speeds when choosing SSDs for your database servers.

- **How:** Consult with hardware vendors or cloud providers to select SSDs that match your database requirements. Consider enterprise-grade SSDs for mission-critical applications.

3. Implement Tiered Storage:

- **What:** Implement a tiered storage strategy that combines SSDs and HDDs.

- **Why:** Not all data requires the speed of SSDs. Tiered storage allows you to allocate SSDs to high-priority data and use HDDs for less critical data.

- **How:** Configure your database server to use SSDs for specific tables, indexes, or transaction logs while using HDDs for archival or less frequently accessed data.

4. Optimize Database Layout:

- **What:** Organize your database to take full advantage of SSDs.

- **Why:** Proper database layout can reduce the number of random I/O operations, further improving performance.

- **How:** Place heavily used tables, indexes, and transaction logs on SSDs. Consider partitioning large tables to distribute data across SSDs efficiently.

5. Monitor and Maintain:

- **What:** Regularly monitor SSD performance and health.

- **Why:** Monitoring helps identify potential issues with SSDs and ensures they are operating optimally.

- **How:** Use SSD-specific monitoring tools or software to track SSD performance metrics like wear leveling and temperature. Implement proactive maintenance, such as firmware updates, to keep SSDs running smoothly.

Real-World Example: Leveraging SSDs in AWS RDS

Amazon Web Services (AWS) Relational Database Service (RDS) offers an excellent example of leveraging SSDs for SQL database performance. AWS RDS provides two types of storage options: General Purpose (SSD) and Provisioned IOPS (SSD).

- **General Purpose (SSD):** Suitable for a wide range of database workloads, this storage type offers a good balance of performance and cost-effectiveness. It uses SSDs for storage.

- **Provisioned IOPS (SSD):** Designed for applications that require the highest level of I/O performance, this storage type allows you to specify the number of IOPS your database needs and uses SSDs as well.

To use these storage options effectively, you can:

- Analyze your database's performance requirements and choose the appropriate storage type.

- Configure the allocated storage to optimize I/O for your specific database workloads.

- Regularly monitor your database's performance metrics, including I/O performance, to ensure it meets your needs.

Conclusion:

Leveraging Solid-State Drives (SSDs) is a powerful strategy for enhancing SQL database performance. SSDs offer unparalleled speed, low latency, and reliability compared to traditional HDDs. By identifying the right workloads, choosing the appropriate SSDs, implementing tiered storage, optimizing your database layout, and maintaining your SSDs effectively, you can significantly boost the performance of your SQL databases. Whether you're managing databases on-premises or in the cloud, SSDs are a crucial tool in your SQL performance tuning arsenal.

PART V
Integration and Performance Testing for SQL

5.1 Leveraging Join Techniques for Enhanced Performance

Join operations are fundamental in SQL database management, allowing you to combine data from multiple tables to derive meaningful insights or generate reports. However, when dealing with large datasets or complex queries, join operations can become performance bottlenecks. In this section, we will explore advanced join techniques and strategies to enhance SQL performance.

Understanding Join Operations:

Before diving into optimization techniques, it's essential to understand the basics of join operations. SQL supports several types of joins, including:

1. INNER JOIN: Returns only the rows that have matching values in both tables.

2. LEFT JOIN (or LEFT OUTER JOIN): Returns all rows from the left table and matching rows from the right table. Non-matching rows from the left table will contain NULL values for right table columns.

3. RIGHT JOIN (or RIGHT OUTER JOIN): Similar to the LEFT JOIN but returns all rows from the right table and matching rows from the left table.

4. FULL JOIN (or FULL OUTER JOIN): Returns all rows when there is a match in either the left or right table. Non-matching rows will contain NULL values for the columns of the table without a match.

Join Optimization Techniques:

Now, let's explore various strategies to optimize join operations for better SQL performance:

1. Indexing: Proper indexing plays a crucial role in optimizing join queries. Ensure that columns involved in join conditions are indexed. Indexes allow the database engine to quickly locate matching rows.

  - **Example:** If you frequently join an "orders" table with a "customers" table on the "customer_id" column, create an index on "customer_id" in both tables.

2. Use the Appropriate Join Type: Choose the right join type based on your requirements. Avoid using a more complex join type (e.g., FULL JOIN) if a simpler one (e.g., INNER JOIN) suffices. Simpler joins are generally faster.

  - **Example:** If you only need records with matching values in both tables, use INNER JOIN instead of FULL JOIN.

3. Limit Result Sets: Minimize the number of rows involved in join operations. Use WHERE clauses to filter data before joining. Reducing the dataset size can significantly improve performance.

  - **Example:** Instead of joining the entire "orders" and "customers" tables, filter orders for a specific date range or customer segment first.

4. Consider Denormalization: In some cases, denormalizing your database by combining related data into a single table can improve join performance. However, this should be done carefully to avoid data redundancy.

   - **Example:** Instead of joining a "products" table with a "categories" table, you could include the "category_name" directly in the "products" table if categories rarely change.

5. Utilize Database-Specific Optimizations: Different database management systems (DBMS) have specific optimizations for joins. Learn about and leverage DBMS-specific features to enhance performance.

   - **Example:** In MySQL, you can use the "STRAIGHT_JOIN" hint to force a specific join order if the query optimizer's choice is not optimal.

6. Analyze Query Execution Plans: Most modern DBMS provide tools to analyze query execution plans. These plans reveal how the database engine executes your query, helping you identify bottlenecks and optimization opportunities.

   - **Example:** In PostgreSQL, you can use the "EXPLAIN" keyword before your query to see the execution plan.

7. Consider Materialized Views: Materialized views store the results of a query as a table, allowing for faster data retrieval. These can be particularly useful for complex joins involving aggregations or calculations.

   - **Example:** If you have a query that frequently joins multiple tables and calculates summary statistics, you can create a materialized view to store the precomputed results.

8. Test and Benchmark: Always test the performance of your join queries with realistic data volumes. Benchmark different join strategies to identify the most efficient one for your specific use case.

- **Example:** Create a test environment that mirrors your production database, populate it with representative data, and measure query performance under various conditions.

Real-World Example: Optimizing E-commerce Product Listings

Consider an e-commerce platform where product listings are stored in a "products" table, and product categories are stored in a "categories" table. Users often search for products within specific categories. To optimize the query that retrieves products within a category, you can:

- Index the "category_id" column in the "products" table for faster category-based filtering.

- Use INNER JOIN to combine product listings with category information, ensuring only relevant products are included.

- Analyze query execution plans to ensure the chosen join strategy is efficient.

- Benchmark the query's performance with different category sizes to validate its scalability.

Conclusion:

Leveraging advanced join techniques is essential for optimizing SQL performance, especially when dealing with large datasets or complex queries. By employing proper indexing, choosing the right join type, limiting result sets, considering denormalization, and using database-specific optimizations, you can significantly enhance the speed and efficiency of your SQL join operations. Remember to analyze execution plans and conduct performance testing to fine-tune your queries for optimal results.

5.2. Building a Performance Testing Environment

A robust performance testing environment is crucial for assessing the scalability, reliability, and efficiency of your SQL database systems. In this section, we will explore the steps to build a performance testing environment, complete with practical examples and best practices.

Why Build a Performance Testing Environment?

Before delving into the details, it's important to understand why a performance testing environment is essential:

1. Realistic Simulation: It allows you to simulate real-world scenarios and user loads to evaluate how your SQL database performs under stress.

2. Identify Bottlenecks: A dedicated testing environment helps identify performance bottlenecks, query optimization opportunities, and potential system weaknesses before they affect your production environment.

3. Capacity Planning: It aids in capacity planning by determining the resources (CPU, memory, storage, etc.) required to support expected workloads.

4. Benchmarking: You can benchmark the performance of different hardware configurations, database designs, or SQL queries to make informed decisions.

Building a Performance Testing Environment:

Follow these steps to build a performance testing environment for your SQL database:

1. Define Testing Objectives:

Start by defining the objectives of your performance tests. What specific aspects of your SQL database are you testing? Is it query response times, concurrency, or scalability? Clear objectives help guide the entire testing process.

Example: Objective: Evaluate the performance of the database under a simulated Black Friday sales event, assessing both query response times and the ability to handle concurrent user traffic.

2. Set up a Dedicated Environment:

Create a separate environment for performance testing. This environment should mirror your production environment as closely as possible in terms of hardware, software, and configurations.

Example: If your production environment uses a Microsoft SQL Server database running on a Windows server, replicate this environment in your testing setup.

3. Populate Test Data:

Generate or import test data that is representative of your production dataset. Ensure that the data volume and distribution mimic real-world conditions.

Example: For an e-commerce platform, populate the testing environment with thousands of product listings, user accounts, and historical sales data.

4. Define Workloads:

Identify the workloads you want to simulate during testing. Workloads can include a mix of read and write operations, complex queries, and transactions that replicate typical user interactions with your application.

Example: Define workloads that include user logins, product searches, order placements, and inventory updates to emulate real user behavior.

5. Configure Monitoring Tools:

Implement monitoring tools to collect performance metrics during testing. These tools should capture CPU utilization, memory usage, disk I/O, query execution times, and other relevant data.

Example: Use tools like Prometheus and Grafana for real-time monitoring and data visualization.

6. Develop Test Scenarios:

Create test scenarios that reflect the objectives and workloads defined earlier. These scenarios should include specific SQL queries, transaction volumes, and user actions.

Example: A test scenario might involve simulating 10,000 users concurrently searching for products and making purchases.

7. Execute Tests:

Run the defined test scenarios in your performance testing environment. Monitor the performance metrics in real-time and record the results.

Example: Execute the Black Friday sales simulation test and monitor the database's response times and resource utilization.

8. Analyze Results:

Analyze the test results to identify performance bottlenecks, scalability issues, or areas for improvement. Look for slow-performing queries, resource constraints, and system failures.

Example: Identify that certain SQL queries experience significant delays during high concurrent user loads, leading to poor user experience.

9. Optimize and Retest:

After identifying issues, optimize your SQL queries, adjust database configurations, or allocate additional resources to resolve bottlenecks. Then, retest to confirm improvements.

Example: Optimize the poorly performing queries by adding appropriate indexes, rewriting SQL statements, or increasing server memory.

10. Document Findings and Recommendations:

Document the findings from your performance tests, along with recommendations for improvements or necessary actions. This documentation serves as a valuable reference for future optimizations.

Example: Create a report that summarizes test results, outlines identified bottlenecks, and provides a roadmap for enhancing database performance.

Best Practices:

Here are some best practices to consider when building and using a performance testing environment for SQL databases:

- **Use Production Data:** Whenever possible, use production-like data to ensure that your tests are as realistic as possible.

- **Automate Testing:** Automate the execution of test scenarios to ensure consistency and repeatability in your tests.

- **Vary Load Levels:** Test under varying load levels, from normal traffic to peak loads, to understand how your SQL database performs under different conditions.

- **Perform Stress Testing:** Conduct stress testing to determine the system's breaking point and assess how it recovers from failures.

- **Monitor Continuously:** Keep monitoring tools running continuously to detect performance issues early, even outside scheduled tests.

- **Secure Test Data:** Protect sensitive data in your testing environment, especially when using production data, to comply with privacy regulations.

Conclusion:

Building a performance testing environment for your SQL database is a crucial step in ensuring the reliability and scalability of your database systems. By following these steps and best practices, you can effectively simulate real-world scenarios, identify performance bottlenecks, and optimize your SQL database for optimal performance and reliability.

5.3. Conducting SQL Performance Testing

SQL performance testing is a critical step in ensuring that your database systems can handle the expected workloads, maintain responsiveness, and meet user demands. In this section, we'll explore how to conduct SQL performance testing effectively, including steps, tools, and best practices.

Why Conduct SQL Performance Testing?

Before diving into the details of how to conduct SQL performance testing, it's important to understand its significance:

1. Identify Bottlenecks: Performance testing helps uncover bottlenecks, such as slow queries, inefficient indexing, or resource constraints, before they impact your application's users.

2. Optimize Queries: By running performance tests, you can identify poorly performing SQL queries and optimize them for faster execution.

3. Evaluate Scalability: Performance testing allows you to assess how your database scales with increasing workloads, helping you plan for future growth.

4. Ensure Reliability: Testing helps ensure that your database system remains reliable and available even under heavy loads.

Conducting SQL Performance Testing:

Follow these steps to conduct SQL performance testing:

1. Define Testing Objectives:

Start by clearly defining the objectives of your performance tests. What specific aspects of SQL performance are you testing? Is it query response times, database throughput, or concurrency handling?

Example: Objective: Assess the response time of critical SQL queries under a simulated user load of 10,000 concurrent users.

2. Identify Key Scenarios:

Determine the critical scenarios that need testing. These could include high-traffic user actions, complex reporting queries, or frequently executed database operations.

Example: Key Scenarios: User login, product search, and order placement.

3. Create Test Data:

Generate or import test data that resembles your production dataset. Ensure that it includes a realistic distribution of data, including various data types and volumes.

Example: For an e-commerce application, create a database with thousands of products, user accounts, and past orders.

4. Develop Test Scripts:

Write test scripts that mimic real user interactions with your application. These scripts should include SQL queries, transactions, and any necessary application logic.

Example: Develop test scripts that simulate users logging in, searching for products, and adding items to their shopping carts.

5. Configure Test Environment:

Set up a dedicated test environment that mirrors your production environment as closely as possible. Ensure that the hardware, software, and configurations match those of your production system.

Example: Use virtualization or containerization to replicate your production database server environment.

6. Define Load Levels:

Determine the load levels you want to test, including the number of concurrent users, transactions per second, or query execution rates.

Example: Test at different load levels, starting from a low traffic scenario and gradually increasing to a peak load scenario.

7. Execute Tests:

Run your test scripts with the defined load levels in your test environment. Monitor the performance metrics, including response times, CPU utilization, memory usage, and database throughput.

Example: Execute tests with 1,000, 5,000, and 10,000 concurrent users, recording response times and resource utilization.

8. Analyze Results:

Analyze the test results to identify performance bottlenecks, slow-performing queries, or resource limitations. Pay attention to deviations from expected performance.

Example: Identify that a specific SQL query experiences a significant increase in response time as the number of concurrent users grows.

9. Optimize and Retest:

After identifying issues, work on optimizing the problematic SQL queries, adjust database configurations, or allocate additional resources to resolve bottlenecks. Then, retest to verify improvements.

Example: Optimize the slow-performing query by adding appropriate indexes or rewriting the SQL statement and then retest under the same conditions.

10. Monitor Continuously:

Even after initial testing, set up continuous monitoring to ensure that performance remains consistent over time. This helps detect any gradual degradation of performance.

Best Practices:

To ensure the success of your SQL performance testing, consider the following best practices:

- **Automate Testing:** Automate test execution to maintain consistency and repeatability.

- **Use Realistic Data:** Ensure that your test data closely resembles your production data to get accurate results.

- **Test Failure Scenarios:** Include scenarios that simulate failures, such as server crashes or network outages, to assess system recovery.

- **Test Security Measures:** Assess how the database handles security measures, like encryption and authentication, under load.

- **Involve Cross-Functional Teams:** Collaborate with developers, database administrators, and system administrators to get a comprehensive view of system performance.

- **Document Test Cases:** Document your test cases, scripts, and results for future reference and audits.

Conclusion:

SQL performance testing is a crucial step in maintaining a high-performing database system. By following these steps and best practices, you can effectively evaluate your database's capabilities, identify and address bottlenecks, and ensure optimal performance for your applications and users.

PART VI
SQL Performance in Production Environments

6.1 Continuous Management and Monitoring of SQL Performance

Once you've tuned your SQL queries and database for optimal performance, your work is far from over. Maintaining SQL performance in production environments is an ongoing process that requires vigilant management and monitoring. In this section, we'll explore the best practices and tools for continuously managing and monitoring SQL performance.

Why Continuous Management and Monitoring is Crucial:

Continuous management and monitoring of SQL performance are essential for several reasons:

1. Early Issue Detection: It allows you to identify performance issues as they arise, preventing them from affecting end-users.

2. Optimization Opportunities: Regular monitoring helps you discover new optimization opportunities as data volumes and usage patterns change.

3. Resource Allocation: You can ensure that resources like CPU, memory, and disk space are allocated efficiently.

4. Capacity Planning: Monitoring helps in capacity planning by providing insights into when and where you might need to scale your database resources.

Continuous SQL Performance Management and Monitoring Process:

Follow these steps to establish a robust process for managing and monitoring SQL performance in production environments:

1. Define Key Metrics:

Start by identifying the key performance metrics you want to monitor. These metrics can include:

- Query response times

- Database throughput

- Resource utilization (CPU, memory, disk I/O)

- Query execution plans

- Index usage

2. Select Monitoring Tools:

Choose appropriate monitoring tools that align with your database system. Many database management systems (DBMS) come with built-in monitoring features, and there are third-party tools available as well.

Example: For SQL Server, you can use SQL Server Management Studio (SSMS) for basic monitoring, or third-party tools like SQL Diagnostic Manager for more advanced capabilities.

3. Set Up Alerts:

Configure alerts based on the selected metrics to notify your team when performance thresholds are breached. Alerts can be sent via email, SMS, or integrated into centralized monitoring systems.

Example: Set up an alert to trigger when query response times exceed 500 milliseconds for a critical application query.

4. Establish Baselines:

Collect performance data over time to establish performance baselines. This helps you understand what "normal" performance looks like for your system.

Example: Monitor query response times over a month to establish a baseline for expected performance.

5. Regularly Review Performance:

Schedule regular reviews of performance metrics and alerts. This can be daily, weekly, or based on your organization's needs.

Example: Conduct a weekly performance review to check for any abnormal spikes in resource utilization.

6. Investigate and Resolve Issues:

When issues arise or performance deviates from the baseline, investigate the root cause. This may involve analyzing slow queries, identifying bottlenecks, or optimizing indexes.

Example: If query response times suddenly increase, use query execution plans to identify inefficient queries and optimize them.

7. Perform Periodic Health Checks:

Conduct periodic health checks to ensure the overall well-being of your database system. This includes tasks like index maintenance, database backups, and updates.

Example: Perform a quarterly health check to defragment indexes and update database statistics.

8. Capacity Planning:

Use historical performance data to predict future resource needs and plan for scalability. This may involve adding more hardware resources or optimizing existing ones.

Example: Based on data growth trends, anticipate when additional storage will be required and plan for expansion accordingly.

9. Document Changes:

Document all changes made to the database, including query optimizations, index modifications, and configuration adjustments. This documentation helps maintain a clear history of system changes.

Example: Create a change log that records the date, description, and impact of each change made to the database.

10. Disaster Recovery Planning:

Include disaster recovery planning in your performance management strategy. Regularly test backup and restore processes to ensure data integrity.

Example: Conduct quarterly disaster recovery tests to simulate data loss scenarios and validate recovery procedures.

Best Practices for Continuous SQL Performance Management and Monitoring:

To ensure effective management and monitoring of SQL performance, follow these best practices:

- **Regularly Review and Adjust Alerts:** Periodically review and adjust your alert thresholds to align with evolving performance expectations.

- **Leverage Historical Data:** Historical performance data is invaluable for trend analysis and capacity planning.

- **Collaborate Across Teams:** Foster collaboration between development, database administration, and operations teams for a holistic view of performance.

- **Automate Routine Tasks:** Use automation tools and scripts to streamline routine tasks like index maintenance and backups.

- **Regularly Update Monitoring Tools**: Keep your monitoring tools up to date to take advantage of new features and improvements.

- **Stay Informed:** Stay informed about the latest updates and best practices for your specific database system.

Conclusion:

Continuous management and monitoring of SQL performance in production environments are essential for delivering a reliable and high-performing application. By implementing a robust monitoring process, promptly addressing performance issues, and planning for scalability, you can ensure that your database system consistently meets user expectations and business needs.

6.2. Dealing with SQL Performance in Production

Once your SQL database is in production, maintaining optimal performance becomes an ongoing challenge. In this section, we'll delve into strategies and best practices for dealing with SQL performance issues in a production environment. We'll cover common performance problems, how to diagnose them, and steps to mitigate their impact.

Common SQL Performance Problems in Production:

1. Slow Query Response Times: Queries that used to perform well can slow down as data grows, impacting user experience.

2. Concurrency Issues: High user concurrency can lead to contention for database resources, causing performance degradation.

3. Resource Contention: Competition for resources like CPU, memory, and disk I/O can result in bottlenecks.

4. Blocking and Deadlocks: Contentious queries can lead to blocking or deadlocks, causing transactional issues.

5. Index Fragmentation: Over time, indexes can become fragmented, affecting query performance.

6. Out-of-Date Statistics: Stale statistics can lead to suboptimal query plans.

7. Resource Exhaustion: Running out of resources like disk space can halt database operations.

Diagnosing SQL Performance Problems:

When you encounter SQL performance issues in production, follow these steps to diagnose the problem:

1. Monitor Performance Metrics:

Use performance monitoring tools to track key metrics like query response times, resource utilization, and transaction rates.

Example: If your monitoring tool reports a sudden spike in query response times, investigate further.

2. Collect Query Execution Plans:

Analyze the execution plans of slow-running queries to identify inefficient query patterns or missing indexes.

Example: Use SQL Server's "Actual Execution Plan" feature to view the execution plan for a problematic query.

3. Check for Locking and Blocking:

Investigate whether blocking or deadlocks are occurring by reviewing database logs and lock-related system views.

Example: Run a query against SQL Server's `sys.dm_exec_requests` view to check for active requests and blocked sessions.

4. Review Database Configuration:

Examine database settings and configurations to ensure they align with best practices for performance.

Example: Check if your database has appropriate memory allocation and file placement.

5. Analyze Resource Utilization:

Look at CPU, memory, and disk I/O usage to identify resource contention.

Example: Use tools like SQL Server's "Performance Monitor" to track CPU and memory usage.

Mitigating SQL Performance Problems:

Once you've diagnosed a performance issue, take the following steps to mitigate its impact:

1. Query Optimization:

Optimize problematic queries by rewriting them, adding appropriate indexes, or using hints to force optimal execution plans.

Example: If a query is performing a table scan, consider adding an index on the filtering column.

2. Index Maintenance:

Regularly perform index maintenance tasks like rebuilding or reorganizing to reduce fragmentation.

Example: Schedule a weekly job to rebuild fragmented indexes.

3. Lock Tuning:

Review and adjust isolation levels and locking strategies to minimize contention.

Example: Change a query's isolation level from "Serializable" to "Read Committed" to reduce locking overhead.

4. Resource Scaling:

Scale hardware resources like CPU, memory, and storage to meet increased demand.

Example: Add more memory to the server to improve overall database performance.

5. Query Caching:

Implement query caching mechanisms to reduce the load on the database for frequently executed queries.

Example: Use a caching framework like Redis to store and serve frequently used query results.

6. Regular Maintenance:

Perform routine maintenance tasks such as database backups, log file truncation, and updates to keep the system healthy.

Example: Schedule daily backups and hourly transaction log backups.

7. Monitoring and Alerts:

Set up proactive monitoring and alerts to catch performance issues before they impact users.

Example: Configure an alert to notify the team when CPU usage exceeds 90% for more than five minutes.

8. Disaster Recovery Planning:

Prepare for potential disasters by implementing robust backup and recovery strategies.

Example: Maintain off-site backups and regularly test the restore process.

9. Capacity Planning:

Analyze trends in resource usage to predict future needs and plan for capacity scaling.

Example: Use historical data to estimate when you'll need to upgrade your database server.

10. Documentation:

Document changes made to address performance issues and maintain a clear record of system modifications.

Example: Keep a log of changes made to query optimizations and their impact on performance.

Conclusion:

Dealing with SQL performance issues in a production environment requires a systematic approach that combines monitoring, diagnostics, and mitigation strategies. By proactively identifying and addressing performance bottlenecks, you can ensure that your database system continues to deliver reliable and high-performance services to your users.

6.3. Navigating and Handling Urgent Performance Issues

In a production SQL environment, urgent performance issues can arise unexpectedly and require quick and effective resolution to minimize downtime and maintain service quality. This section provides a detailed guide on how to navigate and handle such critical situations step by step.

Step 1: Immediate Alert and Identification

Immediate Alert:

When a critical performance issue occurs, the first step is to be alerted promptly. This can be through automated monitoring systems, user complaints, or system administrators.

Identification:

Once alerted, the team must identify the nature and scope of the issue. Common problems include severe slowdowns, outages, or database unavailability.

Step 2: Gather Critical Information

Query or Operation:

Determine which specific queries or operations are causing the performance degradation. Collect the query text, execution plans, and any relevant parameters.

Server Metrics:

Gather real-time server metrics, such as CPU and memory usage, disk I/O, and network traffic. Use performance monitoring tools to collect this data.

Logs and Events:

Check database logs, error logs, and event logs for any unusual entries or error messages that might provide insights into the issue.

User Impact:

Assess the impact on end-users and business operations. Understand how critical the situation is and whether it requires immediate intervention.

Step 3: Triaging and Isolating the Issue

Database or Application:

Determine whether the performance issue is primarily related to the database or if it originates from the application layer. This helps in isolating the root cause.

Query Execution Plans:

Examine execution plans to identify poorly performing queries. Focus on queries with high resource consumption.

Resource Utilization:

Identify any resource bottlenecks, such as CPU, memory, or disk I/O saturation, that might be contributing to the problem.

Locks and Blocking:

Check for blocking and deadlocks that could be hindering database operations.

Step 4: Temporary Fixes and Mitigation

Query Optimization:

If the issue is query-related, consider temporarily optimizing the problematic queries. This can involve adding missing indexes, rewriting queries, or forcing query plans.

Resource Scaling:

If hardware resources are a bottleneck, consider temporarily increasing resource allocation to the database server.

Lock Resolution:

For locking and blocking issues, attempt to resolve them through techniques like killing blocking sessions or adjusting isolation levels.

Step 5: Communication and Incident Response

Notify Stakeholders:

Keep stakeholders, including management and affected users, informed about the situation, progress, and expected resolution time.

Incident Response Team:

Activate an incident response team if one exists, involving database administrators, developers, and system administrators.

Communication Channels:

Establish clear communication channels for incident-related discussions and updates.

Step 6: Root Cause Analysis and Long-Term Fixes

Detailed Analysis:

Perform a detailed analysis to identify the root cause of the performance issue. This may involve examining logs, reviewing query execution plans, and analyzing resource utilization data.

Long-Term Fixes:

Once the immediate issue is resolved, work on long-term fixes to prevent recurrence. This may include query optimization, infrastructure enhancements, or code changes.

Documentation:

Document the incident, including its cause, resolution steps, and preventive measures, for future reference.

Step 7: Testing and Validation

Testing Environment:

Replicate the issue in a controlled testing environment, if possible, to validate the proposed long-term fixes.

Monitoring and Alerting:

Enhance monitoring and alerting systems to proactively detect similar issues in the future.

Step 8: Post-Incident Review

Review Meeting:

Hold a post-incident review meeting with the incident response team to discuss what went well and what could be improved.

Lessons Learned:

Identify lessons learned from the incident and update incident response plans and procedures accordingly.

Documentation Update:

Update documentation with information gained from the incident, including preventive measures and response strategies.

Step 9: Preventive Measures

Automated Monitoring:

Implement or enhance automated monitoring to detect performance issues before they become critical.

Query and Code Reviews:

Enforce regular query and code reviews to catch potential performance bottlenecks early in the development process.

Capacity Planning:

Conduct regular capacity planning to ensure your infrastructure can handle growing workloads.

Conclusion:

Handling urgent SQL performance issues in production environments requires a well-structured approach, rapid response, and a focus on both immediate resolution and long-term prevention. By following these steps, you can effectively navigate critical situations and ensure minimal impact on your organization's operations.

PART VII
Advanced Insights into SQL Performance Tuning

7.1 SQL Performance on Common Database Platforms

SQL performance tuning isn't a one-size-fits-all endeavor. Different database platforms may require unique strategies and considerations for optimal performance. In this section, we'll explore SQL performance tuning on some common database platforms, including MySQL, PostgreSQL, Microsoft SQL Server, and Oracle Database. We'll provide insights, best practices, and platform-specific examples to help you fine-tune SQL performance effectively.

MySQL SQL Performance Tuning

MySQL is a popular open-source relational database management system known for its speed and reliability. When tuning SQL performance on MySQL, consider the following:

1. Indexes: Create appropriate indexes on columns frequently used in WHERE clauses, JOIN conditions, or ORDER BY clauses. Avoid over-indexing, as it can slow down INSERT and UPDATE operations.

Example:

```sql
CREATE INDEX idx_username ON users(username);
```

2. Query Optimization: Use the `EXPLAIN` statement to analyze query execution plans. Optimize queries by selecting appropriate join types, reducing the use of `SELECT *`, and minimizing subqueries.

Example:

```sql
EXPLAIN SELECT * FROM orders WHERE customer_id = 123;
```

3. Buffer Pool Size: Adjust the `innodb_buffer_pool_size` configuration to allocate sufficient memory for caching frequently accessed data. This can significantly improve read performance.

Example:

```ini
innodb_buffer_pool_size = 2G
```

4. Concurrency: MySQL supports different storage engines like InnoDB and MyISAM. InnoDB is recommended for transactional workloads with high concurrency due to its row-level locking.

5. Connection Pooling: Implement connection pooling to reduce the overhead of establishing and closing database connections for each request.

PostgreSQL SQL Performance Tuning

PostgreSQL, often referred to as Postgres, is an advanced open-source database known for its extensibility and SQL compliance. When tuning SQL performance on PostgreSQL, consider the following:

1. Indexes: Create appropriate indexes using the `CREATE INDEX` statement. PostgreSQL supports various index types, including B-tree, GiST, and GIN.

Example:

```sql
CREATE INDEX idx_email ON users(email);
```

2. Query Optimization: Use the `EXPLAIN` statement to analyze query execution plans and identify slow query components. Optimize queries by rewriting, indexing, or adjusting configuration parameters.

Example:

```sql
EXPLAIN SELECT * FROM products WHERE price > 100;
```

3. VACUUM and ANALYZE: Regularly run the `VACUUM` and `ANALYZE` commands to reclaim space and update statistics. Proper maintenance helps keep PostgreSQL performing well.

Example:

```sql
VACUUM FULL;
```

```

```

4. Connection Pooling: Implement connection pooling solutions like PgBouncer to efficiently manage database connections.

Microsoft SQL Server SQL Performance Tuning

Microsoft SQL Server is a widely used relational database system in the Windows ecosystem. When tuning SQL performance on SQL Server, consider the following:

1. Indexes: Create appropriate indexes using the SQL Server Management Studio (SSMS) or SQL scripts. SQL Server provides features like filtered indexes and indexed views.

Example:
```sql
CREATE INDEX idx_last_name ON employees(last_name);
```

2. Query Execution Plan: Use SSMS to analyze query execution plans and identify performance bottlenecks. Adjust queries, add missing indexes, or rewrite SQL statements accordingly.

3. TempDB Optimization: Monitor and optimize the TempDB database, which can become a performance bottleneck during heavy query loads.

4. Max Degree of Parallelism (MAXDOP): Configure the MAXDOP setting to control parallelism. The optimal value depends on your workload and hardware.

5. In-Memory OLTP: Consider leveraging In-Memory OLTP for performance-critical tables and queries.

Oracle Database SQL Performance Tuning

Oracle Database is a powerful and feature-rich relational database system. When tuning SQL performance on Oracle, consider the following:

1. Indexes: Create appropriate indexes using the `CREATE INDEX` statement or through Oracle SQL Developer. Oracle supports various index types, including B-tree and bitmap indexes.

Example:
```sql
CREATE INDEX idx_product_name ON products(product_name);
```

2. SQL Tuning Advisor: Use Oracle's SQL Tuning Advisor to automatically identify and optimize poorly performing SQL statements.

Example:
```sql
-- Run SQL Tuning Advisor for a specific SQL statement
EXEC DBMS_SQLTUNE.CREATE_TUNING_TASK(SQL_ID => 'your_sql_id_here');
```

3. Partitioning: Implement table partitioning to improve query performance, especially for large tables.

Example:

```sql
CREATE TABLE sales
(
    sale_date DATE,
    amount NUMBER
)
PARTITION BY RANGE(sale_date) (
    PARTITION sales_q1 VALUES LESS THAN (TO_DATE('2023-04-01', 'YYYY-MM-DD'))
);
```

4. Automatic Memory Management: Configure Oracle's Automatic Memory Management (AMM) to dynamically allocate memory components, such as the buffer cache and shared pool.

Example:

```sql
ALTER SYSTEM SET MEMORY_TARGET = 4G;
```

These platform-specific SQL performance tuning considerations can significantly impact the performance and efficiency of your database applications. It's essential to understand the unique characteristics and tools available for each database platform and apply best practices accordingly. Regular monitoring, analysis, and optimization are key to maintaining high SQL performance on any platform.

7.2. SQL Performance Tuning for Specialized Applications

In this section, we will delve into the realm of specialized applications and databases, each with its unique requirements for SQL performance tuning. These applications often demand tailored approaches to ensure optimal performance. We will explore three such specialized domains: Geospatial Databases, NoSQL Databases, and Big Data Processing with Hadoop.

Geospatial Databases

Geospatial databases store and manage geospatial data, such as geographic coordinates and shapes. These databases are crucial for applications like geographic information systems (GIS), location-based services, and mapping applications. To optimize SQL performance in geospatial databases, consider the following:

1. Spatial Indexes: Use spatial indexes like R-tree or Quadtree to accelerate spatial queries. These indexes organize geospatial data efficiently for fast retrieval.

Example (PostGIS):

```sql
CREATE INDEX idx_geom ON spatial_data USING GIST(geom);
```

2. Geospatial Functions: Leverage specialized geospatial functions provided by the database engine to perform spatial operations efficiently.

Example (PostGIS):

```sql
SELECT ST_Within(geom1, geom2) FROM spatial_data;
```

3. Clustering: When dealing with geospatial data, clustering data points can reduce the number of calculations and improve query performance.

Example (K-means clustering):

```sql
SELECT kmeans(geom, 5) FROM spatial_data;
```

4. Partitioning: Consider partitioning geospatial data by regions or criteria relevant to your application. This can enhance query performance by reducing the amount of data to scan.

Example (Partition by state):

```sql
CREATE TABLE spatial_data
(
    id serial PRIMARY KEY,
    geom geometry,
    state VARCHAR
)
```

PARTITION BY LIST (state);

```
```

NoSQL Databases

NoSQL databases are designed to handle unstructured or semi-structured data and provide flexibility for rapidly changing data models. Examples include MongoDB, Cassandra, and Redis. When optimizing SQL performance for NoSQL databases, follow these guidelines:

1. Data Modeling: Design your data model according to your application's access patterns. NoSQL databases often require denormalization to reduce the need for complex joins.

Example (MongoDB):

```javascript
// Denormalized data model
{
  _id: 1,
  name: 'John Doe',
  email: 'john@example.com',
  orders: [
    { order_id: 101, total: 50.0 },
    { order_id: 102, total: 75.0 }
  ]
}
```

2. Indexes: Create appropriate indexes for frequently queried fields. In MongoDB, for instance, you can create compound indexes to cover multiple query criteria.

Example (MongoDB):

```javascript
// Create a compound index on 'name' and 'email'
db.collection.createIndex({ name: 1, email: 1 });
```

3. Sharding: NoSQL databases like MongoDB often employ sharding to distribute data across multiple nodes. Proper sharding key selection is critical for even data distribution and efficient query routing.

Example (MongoDB):

```javascript
// Enable sharding for a database
sh.enableSharding('mydb');
// Choose a sharding key (e.g., 'user_id')
sh.shardCollection('mydb.mycollection', { 'user_id': 'hashed' });
```

Big Data Processing with Hadoop

Hadoop is an open-source framework for distributed storage and processing of large datasets. It includes the Hadoop Distributed File System (HDFS) and the MapReduce programming model. SQL performance tuning in Hadoop involves optimizing Hive, a SQL-like query language for Hadoop. Here are some considerations:

1. Partitioning and Bucketing: Partition HDFS data to improve query performance. Additionally, bucketing can help optimize specific types of joins.

Example (Hive):
```sql
CREATE TABLE sales
(
    transaction_id INT,
    product_id INT,
    amount DOUBLE
)
PARTITIONED BY (transaction_date DATE)
CLUSTERED BY (product_id) INTO 4 BUCKETS;
```

2. Vectorized Query Execution: Hive supports vectorized query execution, which processes data in batches rather than row by row. Enable vectorization for performance gains.

Example (Hive):
```sql
SET hive.vectorized.execution.enabled=true;
```

3. Compression and Serialization: Choose appropriate data compression and serialization formats for HDFS data. This choice impacts both storage and query performance.

Example (Hive):

```sql
SET hive.exec.compress.output=true;

SET io.seqfile.compression.type=BLOCK;
```

4. Caching: Utilize Hive query result caching to store intermediate results and accelerate subsequent queries.

Example (Hive):

```sql
SET hive.cache.queryresults=true;
```

Conclusion

Specialized applications and databases require tailored SQL performance tuning strategies. Whether you're working with geospatial databases, NoSQL databases, or processing big data with Hadoop, understanding the unique characteristics and optimization techniques is essential. Always benchmark and monitor your SQL queries to ensure they meet the performance requirements of your specific use case.

7.3. Understanding Performance and Analyzing SQL Source Code

Analyzing SQL source code is a crucial aspect of SQL performance tuning. In this section, we will explore how to gain insights into SQL performance by understanding query execution plans, using profiling tools, and optimizing SQL source code.

Understanding Query Execution Plans

A query execution plan, often referred to as an execution plan or query plan, is a roadmap that the database engine uses to execute SQL queries. It outlines the steps and operations the database will perform to retrieve the requested data. Understanding query execution plans is fundamental to SQL performance tuning.

1. Viewing Execution Plans:

Most relational database management systems (RDBMS) provide tools to view query execution plans. In PostgreSQL, you can use the `EXPLAIN` command:

```sql
EXPLAIN SELECT * FROM employees WHERE department_id = 10;
```

This command will display the execution plan for the given SQL query.

2. Interpreting Execution Plans:

Execution plans consist of nodes representing various operations, such as scans, joins, and sorts. These nodes are connected in a tree-like structure.

- **Table Scan:** A table scan involves reading all rows in a table. It is less efficient than index scans.

- **Index Scan:** An index scan retrieves data using an index, which is generally faster than a table scan.

- **Nested Loop Join:** This type of join involves looping through one table for each row in another table.

- **Hash Join:** Hash joins are used for joining large datasets and involve creating hash tables.

- **Sort:** Sorting operations can be expensive and may indicate the need for proper indexing.

Consider this execution plan example:

```
```

Seq Scan on employees (cost=0.00..20.50 rows=5 width=96)

  Filter: (department_id = 10)
```
```

- The "Seq Scan" indicates a sequential table scan.
- "Filter" shows the filtering condition used.

3. Optimizing Execution Plans:

- **Indexes:** Ensure that tables are properly indexed. In the example above, creating an index on the "department_id" column would improve performance.

- **Query Rewriting:** Sometimes, rewriting a query can lead to a more efficient execution plan. Experiment with different query formulations.

- **Statistics:** Keeping table statistics up to date helps the query planner make better decisions.

Using Profiling and Monitoring Tools

Profiling and monitoring tools provide detailed insights into SQL query performance. These tools help identify bottlenecks, resource usage, and slow queries. Let's explore some common profiling and monitoring techniques:

1. Database Profilers:

Many RDBMSs offer built-in profilers or third-party profilers. For example, in MySQL, you can enable the slow query log:

```sql
SET GLOBAL slow_query_log = 'ON';
```

This logs queries that exceed a specified execution time threshold.

2. Application Profilers:

Application-level profilers track SQL queries initiated by your application code. Tools like New Relic, AppDynamics, or Xdebug for PHP can provide insights into query performance.

3. Query Performance Monitoring:

Use tools like pt-query-digest for MySQL to analyze slow query logs:

```bash
pt-query-digest /path/to/slow-query.log
```

```
```

This tool summarizes query performance metrics, helping you identify problematic queries.

Optimizing SQL Source Code

Optimizing SQL source code involves rewriting queries and making structural changes to improve performance. Here are some optimization strategies:

1. Minimize Joins:

Excessive joins can slow down queries. Consider whether some joins can be eliminated or replaced with denormalized data.

```sql
-- Reduce joins
SELECT orders.order_id, customers.customer_name
FROM orders
JOIN customers ON orders.customer_id = customers.customer_id;
```

2. Avoid SELECT *:

Instead of selecting all columns, specify only the columns you need. This reduces the amount of data transferred.

```sql
-- Avoid SELECT *
SELECT first_name, last_name FROM employees;
```

3. Limit Result Sets:

Use `LIMIT` and `OFFSET` clauses to retrieve only the necessary rows. This is particularly useful for pagination.

```sql
-- Pagination
SELECT * FROM products LIMIT 10 OFFSET 20;
```

4. Optimize Subqueries:

Subqueries can be performance bottlenecks. Rewrite them as joins or consider using common table expressions (CTEs).

```sql
-- Rewrite subquery
SELECT department_name
FROM departments
WHERE department_id IN (SELECT department_id FROM employees WHERE salary > 50000);
```

```
```

5. Use Indexes:

Indexes significantly improve query performance. Ensure that tables have appropriate indexes on columns used in filtering and joining.

```sql
-- Create an index
CREATE INDEX idx_salary ON employees(salary);
```

6. Review Data Types:

Choose appropriate data types to minimize storage and enhance

query performance.

```sql
-- Optimize data types
ALTER TABLE products ALTER COLUMN price TYPE DECIMAL(10, 2);
```

Conclusion

Analyzing SQL source code and query execution plans is vital for SQL performance tuning. Profiling tools and optimization techniques play a critical role in identifying and resolving performance issues. Regularly monitoring and optimizing your SQL code ensures that your database performs efficiently, even as data grows and query complexity increases.

PART VIII
Case Studies and Practical SQL Performance Tuning

8.1 Exploring Real-World SQL Performance Scenarios

In this section, we'll delve into real-world SQL performance scenarios and explore practical solutions for improving database performance. We'll use case studies to demonstrate how to identify, analyze, and resolve SQL performance issues effectively.

Case Study 1: Slow E-commerce Product Search

Imagine you're tasked with optimizing the product search feature of an e-commerce website. Users have reported slow response times when searching for products. Let's go through the steps to address this issue:

1. Gather Data:

Begin by gathering data on slow product searches. Identify which queries are causing the slowdowns and collect query execution plans.

```sql
-- Collect slow query data
SELECT query, execution_time
FROM slow_queries
WHERE query LIKE '%search%';
```

```
```

2. Review Indexing:

Examine the database schema and determine if there are appropriate indexes on columns frequently used in searches, such as product name, description, and category.

```sql
-- Check indexes
SHOW INDEXES FROM products;
```

Ensure that indexes are not fragmented.

3. Optimize Queries:

Rewrite search queries to make use of indexes effectively and avoid full table scans.

```sql
-- Rewrite search query
SELECT product_name, description
FROM products
WHERE product_name LIKE 'keyword%';
```

4. Implement Caching:

Consider implementing caching mechanisms to store frequently accessed search results, reducing the load on the database.

5. Monitor Query Performance:

Continuously monitor query performance to ensure that the changes made have a positive impact. Use profiling tools to identify any remaining bottlenecks.

Case Study 2: High Traffic Social Media Posts

Suppose you manage the database for a popular social media platform, and some posts with high engagement are experiencing slow retrieval times. Let's address this issue:

1. Identify the Problematic Posts:

Identify the specific posts with slow retrieval times and gather data on query execution.

```sql
-- Find posts with slow retrieval
SELECT post_id, retrieval_time
FROM slow_posts;
```

2. Optimize Indexes:

Ensure that the posts table has appropriate indexes on columns used for filtering and sorting, such as post creation date and author.

```sql
-- Check indexes
SHOW INDEXES FROM posts;
```

3. Query Optimization:

Review and optimize the queries responsible for retrieving posts. Avoid using complex subqueries and ensure that joins are efficient.

```sql
-- Optimize query
SELECT post_id, post_content
FROM posts
WHERE author_id = 123
ORDER BY created_at DESC
LIMIT 10;
```

4. Load Balancing:

Implement load balancing to distribute database traffic evenly and prevent overload during peak usage.

5. Use Materialized Views:

Consider using materialized views to precompute and store frequently accessed query results.

Case Study 3: Financial Transaction Processing

Suppose you manage a database for a financial institution, and transaction processing times are critical. Let's explore ways to optimize transaction-related SQL queries:

1. Identify Slow Transactions:

Identify the types of financial transactions that are experiencing delays and collect data on query execution times.

```sql
-- Collect slow transaction data
SELECT transaction_type, execution_time
FROM slow_transactions;
```

2. Database Indexing:

Ensure that tables related to financial transactions have appropriate indexes on account numbers, transaction dates, and other relevant columns.

```sql
```

```
-- Check indexes

SHOW INDEXES FROM transactions;

```
```

3. Transaction Query Optimization:

Optimize transaction-related queries by avoiding full table scans and using efficient join strategies.

```sql
-- Optimize transaction query
SELECT transaction_id, amount
FROM transactions
WHERE account_number = '1234567890'
ORDER BY transaction_date DESC
LIMIT 10;
```

4. Database Partitioning:

Consider partitioning large transaction tables to improve query performance for historical data.

5. Database Replication:
```

Implement database replication to offload read-heavy queries to secondary servers, ensuring that transaction processing is not impacted.

These case studies demonstrate how to address real-world SQL performance scenarios by following a systematic approach: identifying issues, optimizing queries, reviewing indexing strategies, and leveraging caching and other performance-enhancing techniques. SQL performance tuning is an ongoing process that requires constant monitoring and adaptation to ensure your database performs optimally, even under heavy workloads and complex queries.

8.2. Practicing SQL Performance Tuning in Real-Life Situations

In this section, we'll dive into real-life SQL performance tuning scenarios to provide practical insights into addressing complex issues. These examples will guide you through the process of identifying, analyzing, and resolving SQL performance problems effectively.

Scenario 1: Legacy ERP System Slowdown

Background:

You are the database administrator for a company using a legacy Enterprise Resource Planning (ERP) system. Users have been complaining about slow response times when running reports and performing data analysis. The ERP system relies heavily on a SQL Server database.

Steps to Address the Issue:

1. Gather Information:

Start by collecting information about the specific reports or queries that are running slowly. Work with users to determine which tasks are most critical.

```sql
-- Collect slow query data
SELECT report_name, execution_time
FROM slow_reports;
```

2. Database Health Check:

Perform a health check on the SQL Server database. Look for signs of fragmentation, outdated statistics, or issues with the storage subsystem.

```sql
-- Check database health
DBCC CHECKDB ('YourDatabaseName');
```

3. Query Optimization:

Review the slow queries and optimize them. Consider creating appropriate indexes if necessary and ensure that the queries are using parameterization.

```sql
-- Optimize slow query
SELECT *
FROM sales_data
```

```
WHERE date >= '2023-01-01' AND date < '2023-02-01';
```

```
```

4. Monitoring:

Implement monitoring tools to keep a constant eye on the database's performance. Tools like SQL Server Profiler or Extended Events can help you identify bottlenecks.

5. Upgrade or Modernize:

If your ERP system is running on an outdated version of SQL Server, consider upgrading to a newer version. Alternatively, assess whether migrating to a cloud-based solution could improve performance.

6. Load Testing:

Conduct load testing to simulate peak usage scenarios. This will help you identify scalability issues and optimize configurations accordingly.

Scenario 2: ETL Process Bottleneck

Background:

Your organization's ETL (Extract, Transform, Load) process has been running into performance bottlenecks as the volume of data to process has increased significantly. The ETL process uses SQL queries to extract data from various sources, transform it, and load it into a data warehouse.

Steps to Address the Issue:

1. Identify Bottlenecks:

Begin by identifying which stages of the ETL process are causing bottlenecks. Use performance monitoring tools to pinpoint slow-running queries or transformations.

```sql
-- Identify ETL bottlenecks
SELECT stage, execution_time
FROM etl_performance_logs;
```

2. Query Optimization:

Analyze the slow SQL queries used in the ETL process. Look for opportunities to optimize them by rewriting or breaking down complex queries into smaller, manageable parts.

```sql
-- Optimize ETL query
SELECT *
FROM source_data
WHERE date >= '2023-01-01' AND date < '2023-02-01';
```

3. Parallel Processing:

Explore the possibility of parallelizing ETL tasks to leverage multi-core processors. Tools like Apache Spark or SQL Server Integration Services (SSIS) offer parallel processing capabilities.

4. Incremental Loading:

Implement incremental loading strategies to process only new or modified data. This reduces the volume of data to be processed during each ETL run.

5. Data Warehouse Indexing:

Ensure that your data warehouse is properly indexed to support efficient querying. Indexes on frequently used columns can significantly improve ETL performance.

```sql
-- Check data warehouse indexes
SHOW INDEXES FROM data_warehouse_table;
```

6. Resource Scaling:

If your ETL processes are running on cloud-based infrastructure, consider scaling resources up during peak processing times and down during idle periods to optimize costs.

Scenario 3: Web Application Performance Issues

Background:

You are the database administrator for a web-based application that has been experiencing performance issues during high traffic periods. Users have reported slow page load times and occasional timeouts.

Steps to Address the Issue:

1. Identify Slow Queries:

Begin by identifying which SQL queries are responsible for the performance issues. Implement query logging and monitoring.

```sql
-- Log slow queries
SELECT query, execution_time
FROM slow_queries;
```

2. Query Optimization:

Review the slow queries and optimize them for better performance. Ensure that the application uses parameterized queries to prevent SQL injection and improve execution plan caching.

```sql
-- Optimize slow query
SELECT product_name, price
FROM products
```

```
WHERE category = 'Electronics';
```
```
```

3. Caching:

Implement caching mechanisms within the web application to store frequently accessed data. This reduces the load on the database.

4. Connection Pooling:

Configure connection pooling to efficiently manage database connections and reduce overhead.

5. Scaling:

Evaluate the possibility of horizontal scaling by adding more web servers to distribute traffic. Vertical scaling by upgrading hardware or using faster storage can also improve performance.

6. Content Delivery Network (CDN):

Utilize a CDN to serve static assets (e.g., images, CSS, and JavaScript) closer to users, reducing latency.

7. Database Replication:

Implement read replicas to offload read-heavy queries from the primary database, ensuring that transactional performance is not affected.

These real-life scenarios demonstrate that SQL performance tuning is not just about optimizing queries but also involves monitoring, infrastructure adjustments, and thoughtful resource allocation. By systematically addressing performance issues, you can enhance the overall user experience and ensure that your applications and systems perform optimally, even under heavy workloads.

8.3. Scenarios and Sharing Points on SQL Performance Tuning

In this section, we will explore various scenarios and share key insights and strategies for SQL performance tuning. These scenarios are derived from real-world experiences and can help you better understand how to approach and resolve complex SQL performance issues effectively.

Scenario 1: E-commerce Website Slow Checkout

Background:

You manage the database for a popular e-commerce website. During peak shopping seasons, users have reported slow performance when trying to complete their purchases at the checkout. This critical issue affects the website's revenue and customer satisfaction.

Steps to Address the Issue:

1. Identify the Bottleneck:

Start by identifying the specific checkout-related SQL queries that are causing slowdowns. Use SQL profiling or monitoring tools to pinpoint the slowest queries.

```sql
-- Identify slow checkout queries
```

```
SELECT query, execution_time

FROM slow_checkout_queries;

```
```

2. Optimize the Checkout Queries:

Review the slow queries related to the checkout process. Optimize them by ensuring they use appropriate indexes and parameterization. Additionally, consider optimizing complex joins and subqueries.

```sql
-- Optimize slow checkout query
SELECT product_name, price
FROM cart_items
WHERE user_id = ?;
```

3. Caching Strategies:

Implement caching for frequently accessed data, such as product details and pricing information. This can significantly reduce the load on the database during peak traffic.

4. Load Testing:

Conduct load testing to simulate heavy checkout traffic. Monitor database performance during these tests and adjust resource allocation as needed.
```

5. Database Scaling:

Evaluate whether scaling the database by adding more resources or utilizing sharding techniques can alleviate the checkout slowdowns.

6. Error Handling and Logging:

Implement robust error handling and logging mechanisms to capture and diagnose issues during the checkout process.

7. Payment Gateway Optimization:

Collaborate with your payment gateway provider to ensure that payment processing is not causing delays. Optimize integration with payment services.

Scenario 2: Healthcare Patient Record System

Background:

You are responsible for a healthcare application that manages patient records and medical histories. The system has experienced performance issues when querying large datasets, impacting healthcare providers' ability to access patient information efficiently.

Steps to Address the Issue:

1. Identify the Slow Queries:

Begin by identifying SQL queries that retrieve patient records and exhibit slow performance. Focus on queries that involve complex joins or fetch extensive data.

```sql
-- Identify slow patient record queries
SELECT query, execution_time
FROM slow_patient_queries;
```

2. Query Optimization:

Analyze the slow queries and optimize them. Consider creating indexes on columns frequently used in WHERE clauses. Use query execution plans to identify and address performance bottlenecks.

```sql
-- Optimize patient record query
SELECT patient_name, diagnosis
FROM patient_records
WHERE admission_date >= ?;
```

3. Data Archiving:

Implement data archiving strategies to move older patient records to a separate storage or archival system, reducing the size of the active database.

4. Partitioning:

If you are using a database that supports partitioning, consider partitioning large tables based on date ranges or other logical criteria to improve query performance.

5. Concurrency Control:

Implement appropriate concurrency control mechanisms to prevent data contention and deadlocks, especially when multiple users are accessing patient records simultaneously.

6. Monitoring and Alerts:

Set up monitoring and alerting systems to detect performance degradation early. This allows you to proactively address issues before they impact users.

7. User Training:

Train healthcare providers and users to write efficient queries and use search filters effectively to minimize unnecessary data retrieval.

Sharing Points on SQL Performance Tuning:

1. Regular Maintenance:

Perform regular database maintenance tasks such as index rebuilding, statistics updates, and integrity checks to keep your database healthy.

2. Hardware and Infrastructure:

Don't overlook the importance of having an appropriate hardware setup. Ensure that your storage, memory, and CPU resources are sufficient to handle the expected workload.

3. Benchmarking:

Benchmark your SQL queries and database performance regularly to establish performance baselines and identify deviations.

4. Security Considerations:

Incorporate security best practices into your SQL performance tuning efforts. Protect sensitive data and implement authentication and authorization mechanisms.

5. Documentation:

Maintain comprehensive documentation of your database schema, indexes, and query optimization strategies. This documentation can be invaluable for troubleshooting and knowledge sharing.

6. Collaboration:

Collaborate with developers, database administrators, and application teams to address SQL performance issues. Effective communication and teamwork are essential.

7. Review and Feedback:

Continuously review and seek feedback on your SQL performance tuning efforts. Stay open to improvements and keep up with evolving best practices and technologies.

SQL performance tuning is an ongoing process that requires a deep understanding of your application's requirements, database structure, and query patterns. By addressing specific scenarios and sharing key insights, you can enhance your ability to diagnose, optimize, and maintain high-performance SQL databases.

PART IX
The Future of SQL Performance Tuning

9.1 Trends in SQL Performance and Databases

As we delve into the future of SQL performance tuning, it's important to recognize that the database landscape is continually evolving. New technologies, methodologies, and trends are shaping the way we approach SQL performance optimization. In this section, we'll explore some emerging trends and their implications for SQL performance tuning.

1. Data Lakes and Data Warehouses:

Trend: The integration of data lakes and data warehouses is becoming increasingly common. Data lakes store vast amounts of raw data, while data warehouses provide structured, query-optimized access to that data.

Implication: SQL performance tuning will extend beyond traditional databases to encompass data lakes and the interaction between these two storage paradigms. Query optimization strategies will need to consider both environments, and tools will emerge to facilitate cross-environment optimization.

2. Big Data and NoSQL Databases:

Trend: Big Data technologies like Hadoop, along with NoSQL databases like MongoDB and Cassandra, continue to gain traction. They offer scalability and flexibility for handling large, unstructured datasets.

Implication: SQL performance tuning will need to adapt to the unique characteristics of these databases. Techniques for optimizing SQL queries in a NoSQL context will become more critical, and hybrid database solutions may become more common.

3. Cloud Databases and Serverless Computing:

Trend: Cloud-native databases and serverless computing models are on the rise. Services like Amazon Aurora Serverless and Google Cloud Spanner provide scalable, managed database solutions.

Implication: SQL performance tuning will involve considerations specific to cloud-based databases. Auto-scaling, cost optimization, and integration with serverless architectures will be key focus areas.

4. Machine Learning and AI Integration:

Trend: Machine learning and artificial intelligence (AI) are increasingly being integrated into databases. These technologies can optimize query execution plans and suggest indexing strategies.

Implication: SQL performance tuning will leverage AI-driven tools to automate optimization tasks. Database systems will become more self-tuning, leading to improved overall performance.

5. Containerization and Microservices:

Trend: Containerization technologies like Docker and orchestration platforms like Kubernetes are changing the way applications and databases are deployed and managed.

Implication: SQL performance tuning will need to address the challenges posed by containerized database instances. Resource allocation, scaling, and orchestration will play crucial roles in optimizing database performance.

6. Quantum Databases:

Trend: While still in its infancy, quantum computing has the potential to revolutionize database processing. Quantum databases could perform complex queries exponentially faster than classical computers.

Implication: SQL performance tuning may need to adapt to quantum databases in the future, opening up new possibilities for ultra-fast data retrieval.

7. Ethical and Regulatory Considerations:

Trend: As data privacy regulations like GDPR and CCPA become more stringent, ethical and regulatory considerations will impact how databases are designed and queried.

Implication: SQL performance tuning will need to incorporate ethical and compliance-related optimizations. Query auditing, data anonymization, and access control will be essential.

8. Edge Computing:

Trend: Edge computing involves processing data closer to the source, reducing latency and enabling real-time decision-making at the edge of the network.

Implication: SQL performance tuning will need to account for the distributed nature of edge databases. Strategies for optimizing queries in low-latency, high-throughput environments will be vital.

9. Blockchain and Distributed Ledgers:

Trend: Blockchain and distributed ledger technologies are gaining traction in various industries, including finance and supply chain. They provide a tamper-resistant way to store and query data.

Implication: SQL performance tuning will extend to blockchain-based databases, focusing on efficient query processing and consensus mechanisms.

10. Quantum-safe Encryption:

Trend: With the advent of quantum computing, traditional encryption methods could become vulnerable. Quantum-safe encryption algorithms are being developed to address this concern.

Implication: SQL performance tuning will need to incorporate quantum-safe encryption for sensitive data while minimizing the impact on query performance.

Conclusion:

SQL performance tuning is a dynamic field that will continue to evolve as database technologies and data processing paradigms change. Staying informed about emerging trends and adapting SQL optimization strategies accordingly will be crucial for maintaining high-performing database systems in the future. As the database landscape continues to transform, so too will the methods and tools used to ensure SQL query efficiency and overall database performance.

9.2. Predicting and Preparing for the Future

In the fast-paced world of technology and data management, staying ahead of the curve is paramount. As we venture into the future of SQL performance tuning, it's crucial not only to adapt to current trends but also to predict and prepare for what lies ahead. In this section, we will explore some strategies for predicting future trends in SQL performance and how to prepare for them effectively.

1. Continuous Learning and Skill Development:

Prediction: The field of data management and SQL performance tuning is continually evolving with new technologies and techniques. Keeping your skills up-to-date is crucial for anticipating and adapting to future trends.

Preparation: Invest in ongoing training and professional development. Attend workshops, webinars, and conferences focused on database management and SQL performance. Explore online courses and certifications to expand your knowledge base.

2. Benchmarking and Performance Monitoring:

Prediction: SQL performance trends often emerge gradually. By closely monitoring your database's performance metrics and benchmarking against historical data, you can detect subtle changes that may indicate future issues.

Preparation: Implement robust performance monitoring and alerting systems. Use tools like SQL profilers and performance dashboards to track query execution times, resource utilization, and system health. Set up automated alerts to notify you of deviations from baseline performance.

3. Collaboration and Networking:

Prediction: The future of SQL performance tuning may involve solving complex, cross-disciplinary challenges. Collaborating with experts from diverse fields can help you anticipate emerging trends.

Preparation: Attend industry conferences and networking events to connect with professionals from various backgrounds. Engage in knowledge sharing and collaboration to gain insights into future challenges and solutions.

4. Exploring Emerging Database Technologies:

Prediction: New database technologies and platforms will continue to emerge. Some may disrupt traditional SQL databases, while others may complement them.

Preparation: Stay informed about emerging database technologies such as graph databases, time-series databases, and blockchain-based databases. Experiment with these technologies in non-critical environments to understand their potential impact on SQL performance.

5. Automation and AI-Driven Solutions:

Prediction: Automation and AI-driven solutions will play an increasingly significant role in SQL performance optimization, with AI tools assisting in query optimization and index selection.

Preparation: Embrace automation and AI-driven tools for SQL performance tuning. Evaluate and implement AI-powered database management solutions that can help identify and address performance bottlenecks proactively.

6. Hybrid and Multi-Cloud Environments:

Prediction: Organizations will continue to adopt hybrid and multi-cloud strategies, leading to complex data architectures spanning multiple platforms.

Preparation: Familiarize yourself with hybrid and multi-cloud database management techniques. Understand how data can be efficiently and securely transferred between on-premises, private cloud, and public cloud environments.

7. Data Privacy and Security Regulations:

Prediction: Data privacy and security regulations will become even more stringent, requiring robust mechanisms for protecting sensitive information.

Preparation: Stay updated on evolving data privacy regulations and compliance requirements, such as GDPR and CCPA. Implement encryption, access controls, and auditing mechanisms to ensure compliance while minimizing the impact on SQL performance.

8. Quantum Computing Preparedness:

Prediction: Quantum computing, while still in its infancy, has the potential to revolutionize data processing. As quantum technologies mature, they may introduce new challenges and opportunities for SQL performance tuning.

Preparation: Stay informed about developments in quantum computing. Collaborate with researchers and experts in quantum computing to understand its implications for databases. Begin exploring quantum-safe encryption and algorithms to prepare for a quantum-secure future.

9. Ethical and Sustainable Data Practices:

Prediction: Ethical considerations regarding data usage and sustainability concerns will gain prominence. Organizations will need to align their data practices with ethical standards and environmental goals.

Preparation: Advocate for ethical data practices within your organization. Promote responsible data collection, usage, and sharing. Consider the environmental impact of database operations and explore sustainable database solutions.

10. Scenario Planning and Risk Mitigation:

Prediction: The future is inherently uncertain, and unforeseen challenges can arise. Scenario planning and risk mitigation strategies will be essential for adapting to unexpected SQL performance issues.

Preparation: Develop contingency plans and risk mitigation strategies. Conduct scenario-based exercises to prepare for potential disruptions to database operations. Consider factors like data breaches, hardware failures, and natural disasters.

Conclusion:

Predicting and preparing for the future of SQL performance tuning requires a proactive and adaptive mindset. By continuously enhancing your skills, embracing emerging technologies, fostering collaboration, and staying vigilant about potential challenges, you can position yourself as a capable and forward-thinking SQL performance expert. In the ever-evolving landscape of data management, the ability to anticipate and address future trends will be a valuable asset for organizations seeking to maintain high-performing database systems.

PART X
Tools and Software for SQL Performance Tuning

SQL performance tuning is a complex and crucial aspect of database management. While understanding the core strategies and principles is essential, having the right tools and software at your disposal can significantly streamline the process and help you achieve optimal database performance. In this section, we will explore a comprehensive list of tools and software that can assist you in various aspects of SQL performance tuning. We'll provide detailed insights into their features, use cases, and step-by-step instructions on how to leverage them effectively.

1. SQL Profilers:

Description: SQL profilers are essential tools for capturing and analyzing SQL queries executed on your database. They provide valuable insights into query execution times, resource consumption, and query plans.

Use Cases: SQL profiling helps identify slow-performing queries, analyze query execution plans, and pinpoint bottlenecks in your database.

Popular Tools:

   - **SQL Server Profiler (Microsoft):** For SQL Server databases.

   - **pg_stat_statements (PostgreSQL):** A built-in module for PostgreSQL.

   - **MySQL Enterprise Monitor (Oracle):** Provides query performance insights for MySQL databases.

How to Use:

   - Install and configure the profiler tool for your specific database system.

- Set up trace sessions or enable query tracking.

- Capture query data and analyze the results to identify performance issues.

2. Performance Dashboards:

Description: Performance dashboards offer a visual overview of your database's health and performance metrics. They provide real-time monitoring and alerting capabilities.

Use Cases: Performance dashboards allow you to monitor system resource utilization, query performance, and other critical metrics in real-time.

Popular Tools:

- **SQL Diagnostic Manager (IDERA):** Provides a comprehensive performance dashboard for SQL Server.

- **SolarWinds Database Performance Analyzer:** Offers real-time monitoring and performance metrics for multiple database platforms.

How to Use:

- Install and configure the performance dashboard tool.

- Set up monitoring profiles and alerts based on your specific performance metrics.

- Monitor the dashboard regularly to identify and address performance issues.

3. Query Execution Analyzers:

Description: Query execution analyzers help you dive deep into query execution plans, providing insights into how queries are processed by the database engine.

Use Cases: Analyzing query execution plans helps optimize query performance by identifying inefficient operations and missing indexes.

Popular Tools:

- **SQL Server Query Store (Microsoft):** Offers detailed query execution information for SQL Server.

- **EXPLAIN (PostgreSQL/MySQL):** Built-in command to analyze query execution plans.

How to Use:

- Use the appropriate query execution analyzer tool for your database.

- Input the query you want to analyze.

- Review the execution plan to identify performance bottlenecks and optimization opportunities.

4. Indexing Tools:

Description: Indexing tools assist in optimizing database indexes, which are crucial for efficient query processing.

Use Cases: Indexing tools help identify missing or redundant indexes and suggest improvements to enhance query performance.

Popular Tools:

- **SQL Index Manager (IDERA):** Provides recommendations for index optimization in SQL Server.

- **pt-index-usage (Percona Toolkit):** Analyzes index usage in MySQL.

How to Use:

- Install and configure the indexing tool for your database system.

- Run the tool to analyze existing indexes and receive recommendations.

- Implement recommended index changes to improve query performance.

5. Load Testing and Benchmarking Tools:

Description: Load testing and benchmarking tools simulate heavy database workloads to assess performance under stress.

Use Cases: Load testing helps you identify performance bottlenecks, validate scalability, and ensure your database can handle expected traffic.

Popular Tools:

- **Apache JMeter:** A versatile open-source tool for load testing web applications and databases.

- **HammerDB:** Focuses on benchmarking database systems like Oracle, SQL Server, and PostgreSQL.

How to Use:

- Install and configure the load testing tool.

- Define test scenarios and workloads.

- Execute load tests and analyze the results to identify performance limitations.

6. Database Monitoring Solutions:

Description: Database monitoring solutions provide comprehensive insights into database performance, resource utilization, and query performance.

Use Cases: Monitoring tools help you proactively identify and resolve performance issues before they impact users.

Popular Tools:

- **Datadog:** Offers database monitoring for a wide range of database systems.

- **New Relic:** Provides real-time insights into database performance and query analysis.

How to Use:

- Set up database monitoring using the chosen tool.

- Configure alerts and thresholds for key performance metrics.

- Monitor performance dashboards and receive alerts when issues arise.

7. Query Optimization and Tuning Tools:

Description: Query optimization and tuning tools analyze SQL queries and suggest improvements to enhance performance.

Use Cases: These tools help database administrators and developers optimize SQL queries without manually rewriting them.

Popular Tools:

- **SQL Tuning Advisor (Oracle):** Provides SQL statement optimization recommendations.

- **Query Store (SQL Server):** Stores query performance data and provides insights for optimization.

How to Use:

- Input the SQL query you want to optimize into the tool.

- Review the recommendations provided by the tool.

- Apply suggested changes to improve query performance.

8. Database Security and Performance Tools:

Description: These tools offer a combination of security and performance features, helping you ensure your database is both secure and high-performing.

Use Cases: Balancing database security and performance is critical for protecting sensitive data and maintaining optimal performance.

Popular Tools:

- **Imperva SecureSphere:** Provides database security and performance monitoring.

- **Trustwave DbProtect:** Combines database security and performance management.

How to Use:

- Install and configure the security and performance tool.

- Set up security policies and performance monitoring rules.

- Continuously monitor and assess your database for security and performance risks.

9. SQL Code Review Tools:

Description: SQL code review tools analyze database code for potential issues, security vulnerabilities, and performance bottlenecks.

Use Cases: These tools are valuable for ensuring code quality and optimizing queries within applications.

Popular Tools:

- **ApexSQL Enforce:** Offers SQL code analysis and rule-based code testing.

- **Redgate SQL Prompt:** Provides SQL code formatting and analysis.

How to Use:

- Integrate the code review tool into your development workflow.

- Run code analysis on SQL scripts and stored procedures.

- Address code issues to improve performance and security.

10. Database Backup and Recovery Tools:

Description: Backup and recovery tools help safeguard your database and ensure you can quickly restore it in case of data loss or downtime.

Use Cases: Regular backups are essential for data protection and business continuity.

Popular Tools:

- **Veeam Backup & Replication:** Offers backup and recovery for various database systems.

- **Commvault:** Provides comprehensive data protection and recovery solutions.

How to Use:

- Configure regular database backups using the chosen tool.

- Test the restore process to ensure you can recover data when needed.

11. Database Query Caching Tools:

Description: Query caching tools store frequently executed queries in memory for faster access, reducing the load on the database.

Use Cases: Query caching can significantly improve response times for applications with repetitive or identical queries.

Popular Tools:

- **Memcached:** An open-source, high-performance, distributed memory object caching system.

- **Redis:** An in-memory data structure store often used for caching.

How to Use:

- Install and configure the query caching tool.

- Implement query caching logic in your application or database access layer.

12. Database Change Management Tools:

Description: Change management tools help you manage database schema changes, migrations, and version control.

Use Cases: Effective change management ensures smooth transitions between database versions and maintains data integrity.

Popular Tools:

- **Flyway:** Automates database migrations with version control.

- **Redgate SQL Change Automation:** Offers version control, automated deployments, and migration scripts.

How to Use:

- Set up change management processes and workflows.

- Use the tool to create, track, and execute database schema changes.

13. Database Replication and Clustering Tools:

Description: Replication and clustering tools enable database redundancy, failover, and load balancing.

Use Cases: These tools enhance database availability and scalability for high-traffic applications.

Popular Tools:

- **Oracle Data Guard:** Provides real-time data replication and failover for Oracle databases.

- **MySQL Cluster:** Offers automatic sharding and high availability for MySQL.

How to Use:

- Configure replication or clustering settings based on your database system.

- Monitor and maintain replication or clustering for optimal performance.

14. Database Optimization Plugins:

Description: Many database systems offer optimization plugins that can be added to enhance specific performance aspects.

Use Cases: Plugins allow you to tailor your database optimization to your specific requirements.

Popular Tools:

- **Percona Toolkit:** Offers a collection of command-line tools for MySQL optimization.

- **SQL Server Management Studio Extensions:** Various extensions and plugins for SQL Server management.

How to Use:

- Identify the optimization needs of your database.

- Explore and install relevant plugins or extensions.

15. NoSQL Database Management Tools:

Description: For organizations using NoSQL databases, management

tools provide performance monitoring, scaling, and optimization capabilities.

Use Cases: NoSQL database management tools help ensure the efficient operation of distributed and non-relational databases.

Popular Tools:

- **MongoDB Atlas:** A fully managed database service for MongoDB.

- **Cassandra Reaper:** A tool for managing and maintaining Apache Cassandra clusters.

How to Use:

- Deploy and configure the NoSQL database management tool for your specific database system.

- Monitor performance metrics and optimize database configurations.

16. Cloud Database Services and Tools:

Description: Cloud providers offer a range of managed database services and tools that simplify database administration and optimization.

Use Cases: Cloud database services reduce operational overhead and provide scalability options.

Popular Tools:

- **Amazon RDS (Relational Database Service):** A managed database service by AWS.

- **Azure SQL Database:** A fully managed database service by Microsoft Azure.

How to Use:

- Provision and configure the cloud database service based on your requirements.

- Leverage cloud-native tools for performance monitoring and optimization.

17. Custom Scripts and Automation:

Description: Custom scripts and automation can be tailored to your specific database environment and optimization needs.

Use Cases: Custom solutions are ideal for organizations with unique requirements or complex database setups.

How to Use:

- Develop custom scripts or automation workflows to address specific performance tuning tasks.

- Continuously monitor and adjust custom solutions based on evolving needs.

18. Open-Source Tools and Community Resources:

Description: The open-source community provides a wealth of tools, scripts, and resources for SQL performance tuning.

Use Cases: Open-source tools are cost-effective and often customizable to meet your needs.

Popular Tools:

- **pt-query-digest (Percona Toolkit):** Analyzes and reports on MySQL query performance.

- **Database-specific GitHub repositories:** Many open-source projects and utilities are hosted on GitHub.

How to Use:

- Explore open-source tools and scripts relevant to your database system.

- Leverage community forums and resources for guidance and support.

In conclusion, having the right tools and software in your SQL performance tuning toolkit is essential for maintaining a high-performing database environment. Whether you're using commercial solutions, open-source tools, or custom scripts, a well-rounded set of resources will empower you to proactively identify and address performance issues, optimize queries, and ensure the overall efficiency and reliability of your database systems.

PART XI
CONCLUSION

In the ever-evolving world of technology, the performance of SQL databases remains a critical aspect of ensuring that applications run smoothly, meet user expectations, and support business operations. SQL performance tuning is a complex but essential discipline that requires a combination of skills, strategies, and tools. This comprehensive guide has delved into every facet of SQL performance tuning, from understanding the fundamentals to mastering advanced techniques, and from leveraging cutting-edge tools to practicing real-world scenarios.

Throughout this journey, we've explored various aspects of SQL performance tuning, including query optimization, index tuning, database connection management, storage performance, and much more. We've learned about the importance of profiling and monitoring, analyzing execution plans, and optimizing SQL statements for maximum efficiency. We've also discussed the role of performance tuning in production environments and the need to proactively handle urgent issues.

Our exploration extended into advanced insights, such as specialized application tuning and source code analysis, providing a deeper understanding of the diverse challenges one might face. We've also explored real-world case studies, offering practical insights into how SQL performance tuning strategies can be applied in practice.

Looking ahead, the future of SQL performance tuning promises to be dynamic, with emerging trends and technologies influencing the way we optimize databases. Predictive analytics, machine learning, and automation will play increasingly vital roles in proactively managing and tuning database performance.

Thank You:

We would like to express our sincere gratitude to you, the reader, for embarking on this SQL performance tuning journey with us. We hope this comprehensive guide has been a valuable resource in enhancing your skills and understanding in this critical domain of database management.

Your commitment to improving SQL performance is not only beneficial to your organization but also contributes to the broader community of database professionals. As you continue to refine your SQL performance tuning expertise, you're helping to shape the future of database technology.

If you have any questions, feedback, or require further assistance, please don't hesitate to reach out. We're here to support your ongoing journey in SQL performance tuning and database excellence.

Thank you once again for choosing this guide as your companion in the world of SQL performance tuning.

Best regards,

www.ingramcontent.com/pod-product-compliance
Lightning Source LLC
Chambersburg PA
CBHW060536060326
40690CB00017B/3513